STEP-BY-STEP

Quiltmaking

By Barbara Danneman

Golden Press • New York

Western Publishing Company, Inc.
Racine, Wisconsin

A traditional Log Cabin block design patchwork quilt in the Barn Raising pattern, from the collection of Mrs. James Thomson. Light and dark blocks were arranged to form concentric diamonds.

Acknowledgments

I would like to thank my mother, Helen Montgomery, who made the beautiful Cathedral Window quilt. Thanks also to all my friends and colleagues for their help and support; to all the quiltmakers at Riverside Church; to my family, particularly Daniel, Anna, and Ethel Danneman; and to Winifred Bendiner-Viani, Virginia Davis, Carrol Greenbaum, Frances Foster, and Mary Fusco. For special photographs, I am indebted to Ted Becker, Peter Berman, and Bill Wagner, and for the diagrams, to Gary Tong.

Barbara Danneman

Art Director: Remo Cosentino
Art Assistant: Diane Wagner
Diagrams: Gary Tong

Editor: Caroline Greenberg
Associate Editor: Anne-Miriam Hart
Photographs: Remo Cosentino

Library of Congress Catalog Card Number: 74–14090

Contents

Introduction

The art of quiltmaking, once nearly forgotten, has been enjoying a new popularity in recent years, and has now regained its place as an important and accessible craft. The techniques of quiltmaking were originally developed out of necessity. The first quilts were made for warmth, out of scraps of carefully hoarded material, when cloth was precious and hard to come by. Nowadays, with a wealth of machine-made textiles to choose from, we can enjoy quiltmaking for the artistic pleasure it offers, concentrating our efforts on design and execution rather than solely on the practical aspects of the craft.

This book has two aims: to explain the basic techniques of quiltmaking to the beginner and to serve as a reference guide and a source of design ideas for the more experienced quiltmaker. It includes a discussion of materials, descriptions of the different types of quilts, and all the basic steps involved in making a quilt. In addition, there are directions for specific projects, including a sampler, a wall hanging, a pocketbook, and a tablecloth, as well as a variety of quilts.

Quiltmaking is neither complicated nor difficult. It is often said that the best way to learn a craft is to do it, and this is especially true in making quilts. Because quilts are made one step at a time, your skills will grow as your quilt does. The satisfaction of making your own quilt, whether it is a restatement of a grand old design or a completely original one, is sure to establish a long friendship with this unique craft.

HISTORY

The technique of piecing together several layers of cloth to make warm garments probably originated in ancient China and Egypt, but it was not brought to Europe until the eleventh or twelfth century, when knights returning from the Crusades in the Middle East came back to Europe wearing quilted patchwork vests under their armor. The happy discovery that thick, quilted garments provided more warmth than single layers of clothing was quick to spread in Europe, and coincided with a sudden shift to a colder climate in western Europe during the thirteenth and fourteenth centuries.

Because at this time cloth was painstakingly woven by hand, the scraps that were pieced together to make clothing and bed covers were used with an eye to function rather than design. As new kinds of cloth came to Europe via the Eastern trade routes opened up by the Crusades, quiltmaking gradually became a refined domestic craft. The fifteenth, sixteenth, and seventeenth centuries saw the development of distinct regional styles of quilts. In northern Europe and Britain, warm, sturdy quilts of wool and homespun were made in simple geometric designs. Finer quilts from this area were made of plain linen combined with figured chintz; these were often

A mid-nineteenth century English coverlet from the Victoria and Albert Museum collection. Applied motifs of stylized animals and figures in printed cottons on a white cotton background.

Detail of a traditional block design patchwork quilt, Storm at Sea, by Virginia Davis. Squares and diamonds of the same print in three different colors give a harmonious, one-textile look to the quilt. Red and green, complementary colors, are a favorite combination of quiltmakers.

embroidered with scrolls and floral patterns. In southern Europe, where warmth was not an important consideration, quilts were made of fine, lightweight fabrics and were elaborately embroidered, often with raised designs. In both northern and southern Europe, many families developed their own distinctive designs for quilts. These were passed down from mother to daughter as family heirlooms.

As factory-made goods became more accessible toward the end of the eighteenth century, fewer quilts were handmade in Europe. In the New World, however, where industrial progress was slower, the tradition of quiltmaking flourished. Though few quilts remain from this period, inventories made by the settlers show that quilts were a standard item in baggage brought over to America.

Quiltmaking began as a necessity for the pioneers. At first, scraps of hand-woven and hand-dyed fabric were sewn together in any sort of order to make warm coverings. As the hardships of pioneer life and the short supply of cloth eased, American quilt designs became more refined and developed their own unique American character. In later years the quilting bee became a popular social institution, and the development of a national spirit led to the appearance of countless patterns that reflected the American scene. New patterns developed as new localities were settled, and quiltmaking became a welcome recreation.

Quiltmaking in America has never really died out. There have always been quiltmakers in the United States, particularly in rural areas, but recently a new appreciation of the artistic value of quilts

This lined, unquilted patchwork spread by Frances Foster shows a striking use of African prints that combine to make a rich design.

"L.A." 1969. A contemporary black, white, and sepia tie-dyed panel, designed, dyed, and quilted by Joanne Brandford.

has helped to make it an urban craft as well. The development of new textiles, the ecology movement and its emphasis on conservation and recycling, and the current interest in individual expression through craft work add to the exciting possibilities of quiltmaking.

HOW TO BEGIN

This book begins with a glossary of quiltmaking terms, a description of different kinds of quilts, and information about equipment and cloth. There is a general section on design, drafts, patterns, cutting, sewing, quilting, and binding—all the steps involved in making almost any sort of quilt. The various projects, including a detailed explanation for making the Around the World quilt, illustrate many different aspects of quilt construction.

Following the construction of a quilt from start to finish is a time-tested way of learning the craft; traditionally, quiltmaking was learned in the home, by observation. The illustrations and explanation for making the Around the World quilt, which begin on page 47, are meant to give you an idea of the basic step-by-step quiltmaking process. Reading through the section Basic Steps and Techniques for quiltmaking (see page 23) and then reading the directions and looking at the illustrations for the Around the World quilt will acquaint you with the basic steps for making almost any kind of quilt. After you have learned the basic techniques, you can begin a quilting project of your own, either by following the instructions given for the project you choose, or by adapting specific directions to your own design. Quiltmaking is an old craft, but not an inflexible one. You will be free to use any one of hundreds of traditional designs, or to combine traditional design elements with original ones. Because the opportunity to use personal design is one of the most delightful aspects of quiltmaking, the emphasis of this book is on design rather than technique.

SEWING

The decision of whether to sew your quilt by hand or by machine is entirely up to you and will depend on your sewing experience. The sewing machine is a wonderful tool for quiltmaking but certainly not an essential one. Traditionally, of course, quilts were sewn by hand, but using a machine offers the advantages of speed and greater durability. The instructions in this book for machine sewing assume that the reader has enough experience in sewing by machine to sew straight, accurate seams.

Hand sewing in quiltmaking has its advantages too. Even if you have had little experience in sewing by hand, all you really need to know for most hand-sewn quiltmaking projects is how to do a simple running stitch. Hand sewing can also be more accurate than machine sewing and will allow you to take your quilt with you so that you can work on it in the company of friends, or at odd moments.

The general rule is that long seams and large pieces are better done by machine, and smaller or curved pieces are better done by hand.

QUILTMAKING TERMS

The following are terms that are used by quiltmakers to describe various aspects of the craft, and they are used throughout this book.

Quiltmaking: the name for the entire process of making a quilt.

Quilting: the basic method of connecting the two or three layers of a quilt by sewing them together, usually done by using small, even stitches in a decorative design. Quilting can be done by hand or on a sewing machine. (Other methods of connecting the layers of a quilt, such as tying, are described on page 42.)

Top: the upper side of a quilt.

Filling: the substance between the top and the back of the quilt. (Some quilts do not have a filling.)

Back: the lining or underside of a quilt.

Pattern: the guide for each piece of fabric in a quilt. (A pattern may be made of paper, cardboard, sandpaper, or clear plastic.) Also, a quilt design, such as the Puss in the Corner pattern.

Patch: a single unit or piece of cloth.

Piece: a patch. Also, to sew patches together.

Block: a unit of patches; either one complete design unit or a section of the top broken down for ease in handling.

Setting: the process of sewing blocks together.

Lattice strips: bars of cloth between blocks.

Border: cloth that is sewn around the central design of the quilt. Borders may be plain or decorative.

Binding: the process of finishing off the edges of the quilt. Also, the material used to enclose, or bind, the unfinished edges of a quilt.

This late nineteenth century nine-patch patchwork quilt in the Puss-in-the-Corner pattern illustrates patches, blocks, diagonal lattice strips, decorative borders, and binding.

Kinds of Quilts: A Preview

Quilts fall into two basic categories, depending upon how the top of the quilt is constructed. The first type has a pieced top, made of many patches of fabric, and is called a patchwork quilt. The second has a one-piece or appliquéd top; appliqué quilts, crazy quilts, and trapunto quilts fall into this category. The top of an appliqué quilt consists of one piece of fabric to which smaller pieces of fabric have been appliquéd, or "laid on," leaving areas of the background material visible. The top of a crazy quilt has a backing that is entirely covered by pieces of fabric appliquéd or laid on to it. The one-piece top of a traditional trapunto quilt is sewn to the back of the quilt with stitching that outlines a small pictorial area, or with parallel lines of stitching that form a design. Certain areas of the design are then filled with cording or stuffing by means of slits in the back, creating a raised effect.

In all types of quilts the design of the top is paramount, but it is also important to consider how the layers of the quilt are assembled and finished. Traditional construction is like a sandwich—the top and the back enclose the filling—and the three layers (or in some cases only two, a top and a back) are connected either by hand or machine stitching (quilting), or by tying. In the tying method, the top, filling, and back are joined together with tied or knotted cotton or wool yarn. Less conventional quilts may be assembled in sections, or assembled after each individual patch or block has been stuffed.

Both kinds of quilt designs—pieced tops and one-piece tops—are discussed and illustrated on the following pages, with suggestions for methods of construction.

Lone Star, a late nineteenth century center motif patchwork quilt of cotton and calico. University of Kansas Museum of Art, The William B. Thayer Memorial.

Quilts with Pieced Tops

Block Designs

Block designs originated in England, and were brought to America by the first settlers. During the nineteenth century, block designs with such names as Road to California, Virginia Star, Steps to the Altar, Log Cabin, Kansas Troubles, Old Tippecanoe, and Corn and Beans were created. Though the titles are wildly romantic and hint at complexity, the blocks themselves are simple enough to re-create. One widely-used method for re-creating such traditional designs is to take a square piece of paper, fold it into sections, and then join up points on the folds with straight lines to make patterns for the block. (See page 25 for a fuller description of this method.) Common divisions of a block are into four squares, known as four-patch, sixteen squares, known as sixteen-patch, and nine squares, known as nine-patch.

Blocks are made separately and put aside until all are finished. They may then be set in a variety of ways—next to one another, alternating with plain blocks, or alternating with lattice strips. Block designs may be set by hand or by machine. The traditional method of quilting block design quilts is by hand. However, they can be quilted by machine, or connected by tying. The Log Cabin block design, for instance, is traditionally tied rather than quilted.

A complete explanation for making the Around the World quilt begins on page 47. Instructions for making three other block design projects, a Log Cabin pocketbook and tablecloth and a Georgetown Circle pillow cover, begin on page 52.

Allover Designs

A patchwork allover design quilt has one pattern shape that repeats over and over again. Shapes such as squares, triangles, rectangles, or hexagons may be pieced randomly, or in a design that results from the planned juxtaposition of different colors of cloth. Allover designs can be done successfully with a limited palette: Early American quilts were often only blue and white or red and white. Or designs can be created by the placement of the brightest or darkest pieces so that they stand out to form a pattern.

An allover design is a good choice for a charming but uncomplicated quilt. The plan can be simple, and the construction may be carried out in a number of ways. The most traditional way of making an allover design quilt is to piece the entire top; however, the quilt can be quilted in sections and then assembled, or assembled after each block or patch has been stuffed individually. The allover design quilt pictured on page 22 is hand quilted on the inside of each hexagonal piece, but this sort of treatment is not necessary for less formal quilts. Many allover design quilts can be tied rather than quilted.

Instructions for an allover design quilt of random-color squares are given on page 58, and directions for making an allover design quilt of pre-stuffed triangles are given on page 61.

Center Motifs

Center motif quilts have a design that begins from a central point. Stars, sunbursts, and decorative medallions or panels are some of the most widely-used center motifs.

Of all the kinds of patchwork quilts, the star-pattern quilt is considered a masterpiece. The design is one that requires careful planning at every stage—from the exact fit necessary for each diamond-shaped piece to the total blending of colors radiating from the center of the pattern. The design for a star quilt can be duplicated from an existing quilt, but to allow for more flexibility, an exact plan can be drafted from the dimensions of the single diamond-shaped motif, which is repeated over and over to form the star. Unquilted stars are perfect for pillow covers or a round tablecloth; when quilted, with every diamond-shaped patch outlined, a star quilt or wall hanging makes one of the most spectacular patterns.

Other types of center motifs are the central panel and medallion. During the nineteenth century, a printed central panel or embroidered medallion was often specially prepared to celebrate an important event. It would then be surrounded with decorative borders or frames to make an entire quilt, like the one shown on page 32. Some contemporary combinations of embroidery and patchwork have revived this interesting and creative approach to quiltmaking.

A star quilt is pictured on page 8. Instructions for making a star-pattern wall hanging are given on page 64.

Irregular Designs

Traditionally, patchwork quilts were made with a unit design plan that repeated over the entire top. However, patchwork quilts without any repeat plan have always been made. In the past, these were used as "everyday" quilts, and they were made up from left-over dressmaking scraps and the usable portions of old clothes. The designs and the type of quilting used were dictated by the choice of odd bits of fabric at hand. These irregular designs were often composed of squares, rectangles, and stripes that were pieced together. Quiltmakers of the past no doubt enjoyed this creative sort of endeavor just as much as modern quiltmakers do; the opportunity to make up original designs with cloth is always an exciting one.

The difference between irregular design quilts and crazy quilts is in the way they are sewn. Irregular design quilts are patchwork —shapes are pieced together to form the quilt's top. Crazy quilts (see page 13) are made of irregularly shaped pieces of fabric that are appliquéd or laid on to a one-piece backing; the backing is entirely covered by the pieces.

Instructions for making an irregular design patchwork quilt are given on page 68.

An irregular design striped patchwork quilt by Winifred Bendiner-Viani. Cotton print rectangles were cut and arranged to please the eye, without a pre-planned design.

Cathedral Window Quilts

The Cathedral Window method is an ingenious way to make a patchwork-style quilt without taking any of the traditional steps. The Cathedral Window is unique because it has neither a filling nor a backing, but looks as if it were quilted nonetheless. The quilt is made of folded plain cloth squares that make "frames" for its colored or printed cloth "windows." The method of folding resembles Japanese origami, but no one really knows the origin of the technique. Each plain square is folded separately; units of these folded squares, when connected, comprise the entire quilt surface, both top and back. When the colorful print windows are sewn in, the stitches go through all the folded layers of the frames, making quilting.

Because the Cathedral Window must be sewn entirely by hand, it is a good project to work on at odd moments. You might enjoy making a Cathedral Window quilt as an unhurried, long-term project. A pillow or a sampler is a good smaller project to try. And if you sew the folded squares together with a double strand of thread, you can make a sturdy shopping bag or pocketbook that will need no additional lining.

Detailed instructions for making a Cathedral Window quilt begin on page 70.

(Below) Three pocketbooks, clockwise from upper left: Variable Star block design by Catherine Josi (instructions for making this style of pocketbook are given on page 52); Cathedral Window with crocheted strap by Fumiko Ueno; patchwork squares with embroidery by Diane Wagner. (Below right) Detail of Cathedral Window quilt by Catherine Josi. The folded squares are set so the edge of the quilt is straight, rather than saw-toothed.

Quilts with One-piece and Appliquéd Tops

Appliqué Quilts

Appliqué quilts are composed of cloth cutouts that are sewn onto a one-piece top, or onto blocks that are then assembled to make the top. Many beautiful quilts in American museums today are examples of appliqué work, in which the traditional designs of flowers, birds, hearts, and baskets of fruit are used. Since appliqué quilts were often thought of as "special," and were frequently sewn to commemorate marriages, births, and other important occasions, they were almost always made by the most skilled quiltmakers. The finest materials were used, and great care went into the selection of color and design. Most appliqué quilts have large open areas for elaborate quilting. Designed to complement the appliqué, the quilting is often so lavish and rich that it creates a beautiful pattern in its own right.

Modern appliqué quilts may be made with larger-than-traditional designs, abstract designs, or motifs cut from printed goods. Although appliqué quilts are traditionally made by hand, attachments on newer sewing machines make appliqué by machine possible.

Directions for an appliqué sampler are given on page 46, and for an appliqué presentation quilt, on page 77.

Crazy Quilts

A crazy quilt is composed of odd-shaped scraps of material that overlap or fit together like a jigsaw puzzle and are appliquéd onto a base so that the backing is completely covered. Perhaps the most fanciful quilts of the Victorian age were the crazy quilts, which were made up of odd bits of velvet, brocade, silk, and satin, and embellished with fine embroidery that gave them unusual, collagelike designs. Usually the scraps were appliquéd onto small blocks of material; the blocks were then joined together with strips of cloth, ribbon, or more embroidery, and a lining was added.

This technique of assembling bits of cloth and sewing them onto a fabric base is not a new one. It dates from medieval times, when cloth was so valuable in Europe that scraps were saved and sewn together to make warm coverings. Later, when cloth was more accessible and needlework more refined, the technique was used decoratively. The Victorians seized on it as a way to use slippery, stretchy fabrics that are difficult to piece in any other way.

The crazy-quilt method is an attractive one because it offers the craftsperson the opportunity to combine colors and textures in an original way. The sewing and outlining of the pieces may be done by hand or with various kinds of machine embroidery stitches.

Instructions for a crazy quilt wall hanging are on page 73.

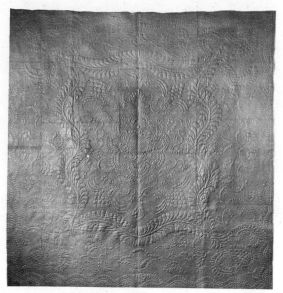

A traditional late nineteenth century homespun linen trapunto quilt in the flower basket pattern. University of Kansas Museum of Art, The William B. Thayer Memorial.

Trapunto Quilts

Trapunto is the name for a bas-relief quilting method that originated in southern Europe and became popular in the United States in the nineteenth century. In traditional trapunto, a design is sewn through the top and back of the quilt (there is no filling), and then certain areas of the design are stuffed to raise and accentuate the pattern. The traditional trapunto quilt is one color, usually white, and the designs are similar to classic appliqué patterns, such as flowers and baskets of fruit.

The process begins with a design that is drawn in pencil onto the quilt top. The top and back are then basted together, and the pattern is outlined with a double row of very small running stitches. Bits of filling or cording are inserted between the stitching through small slits cut in the back, and the slits are then carefully mended.

Real skill and care are needed for making flawless trapunto quilts. While the technique remains interesting, the classic motifs seem slightly out of date today. Free-flowing hand or machine stitching offers unlimited possibilities for bas-relief soft-sculpture effects because the filling, added at the end, is not an encumbrance during the quilting.

Directions for making a modern adaptation of a trapunto-style quilt are given on page 74.

Presentation and Friendship Quilts

A traditional presentation or friendship quilt was a group project, and usually marked a special occasion such as a marriage, birth, graduation, or the commemoration of an event. A presentation quilt might also have been a highly personal gift given to someone who had been of great service to an organization such as a church, club, or hospital. Appliqué blocks were designed and sewn by different people, each block in the quilt illustrating some aspect of the donor's life. Often the block was signed by its maker. For example, graduating school girls might have appliquéd squares, signed them, and exchanged them with all their friends. When the squares were connected, each quilt would be a grand remembrance of school days. The Abraham Lincoln Spread shown on page 16 was probably made at a quilting party. Each donor recorded his interests or political sympathies in the quilt.

Presentation quilts generally had one theme, and another unifying aspect, such as lattice strips or a limited color scheme, to give the quilt a harmonious appearance. The appliqué designs were pictorial, stylized, and very charming. Often, the individual blocks were presented at the special occasion to be commemorated or at a public ceremony. Sometimes the blocks would be set by the same people who had made them, after they had been presented. Those who were considered the best quilters would then be responsible for the quilting.

A presentation quilt is pictured and described on page 77.

Detail of an appliqué and embroidery presentation quilt made to honor the outgoing president of a college by his friends and colleagues. Owned by Dr. and Mrs. Ralph C. John; photo by Robert P. Boner.

A Martindale pattern appliqué quilt. Loaned by The Denver Art Museum, Denver, Colorado. Gift of Mrs. Charlotte Jane Whitehill.

Crazy quilt from the collection of Mary Polinsky. Warm tones of wool, satin, and velvet, with embroidery.

Abraham Lincoln presentation quilt. This spread is made of 49 squares of cotton and homespun linen, each appliquéd with a different design and signed by its maker. Note the wonderful Abraham Lincoln portrait in the upper-right center of the quilt. From the Shelburne Museum, Inc., Shelburne, Vermont.

Equipment and Materials

EQUIPMENT

The following is a list of the basic tools for quiltmaking. For the most part they are ordinary sewing materials. Assemble them in a basket and keep them with your quilt as you work on it.

1. Scissors. Barber's shears are best, but whatever sort you use, they should be sharp. Keep a pair of scissors just for cutting cloth and another for cutting paper, cardboard, and plastic patterns. (Pinking shears are never used for quiltmaking.)

2. Thread. Number 50 cotton thread is used for most quiltmaking. There is also a special thread for quilting that resists tangles.

3. Hand sewing needles. Number 8, 7, or 6 sharps or millinery needles are good.

4. Lightweight cardboard, sandpaper, or clear plastic for patterns. Heavy paper for patterns that will only be used a few times.

5. A ruler for marking straight lines on patterns or fabric.

6. Straight pins.

7. Carbon paper for transferring patterns from paper to cardboard.

8. Paper for drawing blocks or for calculating yardage requirements. (Newspaper is fine.)

9. Graph paper for making drafts. Ten squares to the inch is an easy size to work with.

10. A compass, or a pencil with a string attached to it, for making circles.

11. Pencils for drawing patterns, marking cloth, and so on. A light dressmaker's pencil for marking on dark cloth. A ball-point pen for marking light-colored cloth, for tracing patterns on clear plastic, and so on.

12. An iron, preferably a steam iron.

13. A sewing machine (optional). The advantages and disadvantages of using a machine rather than sewing and quilting by hand are discussed on page 6.

The equipment you will need for quilting depends on the quilting method you choose; see the section on Quilting, page 36.

FABRICS FOR THE TOP

Your choice of cloth is vast, and you can use just about anything from cottons to snips of fur to make your quilt—creative quiltmakers have even used labels from clothing. When choosing fabric, however, consider its weight and thickness carefully. Fabrics of unequal weight and thickness are not usually used together when making a quilt with a pieced top, as heavy fabric will pull lightweight fabric out of line.

A work basket and equipment. Patches for the Around the World quilt (see page 47) are stacked in groups of ten for easy handling and keeping after the pieces have been hand stitched.

(Right) Detail, Philadelphia Pavements, by Diane Wagner. A nine-patch block design cotton patchwork coverlet with lattice strips.

(Below) A hand-quilted patchwork quilt in different colors of the same calico print, by Elizabeth Hopkins. To make this simple, innovative design, squares of calico were cut into four triangles, and long pieces of calico were cut into strips of unequal width. The pieces were then reassembled, according to color, to please the eye. (See Cutting without Patterns, page 30.)

Cottons, such as calico prints, broadcloth, gingham, muslin, and percale, are all excellent, as they do not fray or stretch, and they are easy to sew. Denim is good to use, as is glazed chintz, which is particularly attractive in combination with flat-surfaced cotton.

If you want to make a heavy quilt, consider using materials such as corduroy, sailcloth, velvet, or wool.

Attractive quilts have been made from African printed cotton, hand-blocked and hand-dyed cloth, ribbons, and braids. The variety is endless.

Silks are traditional for crazy quilts, and they look beautiful when they are pieced into geometric blocks. Piecing silk is difficult unless it is reinforced; otherwise it will slip and fray. The best way to overcome this problem is to back silk with a lightweight iron-on bonding material, such as Shape-Flex or Stitch-Witchery. If you combine any washable materials with silk, velvet, or fur, your quilt will have to be dry-cleaned. Wool is washable in cold water.

Synthetic blends such as polyester and cotton, and dacron and cotton, though they lack the wonderful texture of 100 percent cotton cloth, require little ironing before or during sewing, and always look crisp. Cotton blends have become so popular in recent years that they are now more readily available than pure cotton.

Unsuitable fabrics. Heavy, stretchy, or flimsy materials such as burlap, hopsacking, terry cloth, duck, and jersey are difficult to piece together. Almost any kind of cloth may be used, however, if it is appliquéd to a backing.

MATERIALS FOR THE FILLING

The filling you use will depend on how you want to use your quilt, how you want it to look, and how warm you want it to be. The most popular filling for quilts today is dacron polyester fiberfill, which is available in most department stores in ¼-inch thick sheets cut to standard quilt sizes. (Be sure not to buy bags of shredded dacron.) Dacron resembles cotton batting, but it is lighter in weight, easier to stitch through, and superior to cotton batting because it is machine washable and will not bunch in automatic dryers. It is now made with an invisible resin bonding that holds it together better than the grid of stitching in older kinds of filling.

If you want to make a very lightweight quilt, you can peel down the dacron filling to less than its ¼-inch thickness or use thin cotton flannel or a thin blanket as a filling. Or, if you'd like to make a heavy, puffier quilt, you can use two sheets of dacron filling stacked together, or a thicker type of dacron polyester fiberfill available in commercial quiltmaking shops.

FABRICS FOR THE BACK

The back, or lining, of your quilt should be made of a fabric that is easy to stitch through. Most fabrics that are fairly loosely woven, such as muslins, cottons, cotton blends, and cotton flannel, are easy to hand quilt. Corduroy makes a sturdy back and is suitable if you plan to tie or machine quilt your quilt.

Most yard goods are 36 or 45 inches wide. If you want to make a back without a seam running lengthwise down or across its middle, use a cotton, muslin, or flannel sheet. India print or homespun bedspreads also make excellent backs. Otherwise, two lengths of yard goods joined at the center are perfectly acceptable.

SOURCES FOR MATERIALS

The most obvious place to go for fabric is the fabric store. However, if you need a large selection of small amounts of different prints or colors, bear in mind that most fabric stores do not like to sell less than ¼ yard of any fabric. Stores selling remnants, samples, or discontinued fabrics, on the other hand, are excellent sources of small quantities of cloth. Another good source is friends who sew—ask them to save leftover cloth for you.

As the history of quiltmaking shows, it is not at all necessary to make quilts from new fabric. Old sheets, neckties, and clothing can all be cut up and used in quilts, providing the fabric is in good condition.

PREPARING THE CLOTH

It is a good idea to wash and dry all the washable cloth you plan to use in your quilt before you begin cutting. The cloth will look and feel better, excess dye will be removed, and different shrinkage rates will cease to be a source of worry.

Use hot water and the hot setting on the dryer, and be sure to test cloth that runs. If the cloth continues to run, do not use it unless you plan to dry-clean your quilt. Iron any rumpled material before you cut your patterns.

(Facing page) Patchwork quilt by Judy Flaxman. Note the effective color-blending of the small square patches, set off by black framelike borders, in this handsome quilt.

Grandmother's Flower Garden, a hand-quilted, allover design in hexagons. Note how the medallions form an attractive scalloped saw-tooth edge. From the collection of Ethel Danneman.

Basic Steps and Techniques

CHOOSING A DESIGN

Choosing a design is the first step in making a quilt. It is also one of the most important—the design of any quilt is what makes it outstanding. If you are about to begin your first quilt and are having difficulty choosing a design, decide first whether you'd rather use a traditional design or an original one. In addition to the traditional designs in this book, you can find examples in other books, in museums, and in the catalogs of quilt pattern suppliers. (Many of the suppliers listed on page 80 carry quilt patterns.)

If you would rather create your own design than use an old one, experiment with colored paper or with fabrics and put together sample blocks (design units) in various combinations of colors. Look at fabric designs, tile designs, wallpaper, tapestries, and abstract paintings—all are potential sources of interesting patterns. Whatever you choose as your first design, make sure it is not overly complicated or difficult. A simple patchwork or appliqué design would be ideal.

COLOR AND DESIGN CONSIDERATIONS

Quiltmaking is an activity that offers exciting possibilities for the use of color and design. As a quiltmaker, you will deal with bits of fabric as if they were paint, and work with the sculptural effects of quilting as they relate to your design. Fortunately, you will have ample opportunity to decide (and to change your mind about) how you'd like your quilt to look; one of the great advantages of quiltmaking is that you can envision and then draft a design, cut out the pieces, and then lay them out to see how they look before you begin sewing your quilt (see photos on pages 34 and 50). If the effect is not pleasing to the eye, you can rearrange the pieces in a variety of ways.

As part of a room's furnishings, a quilt should either blend in with the colors in the room or pick up and accent certain colors. Multi-color patchwork tends to blend with almost every color, as will a design composed of colors in the same tonal range. That is, a quilt made up of medium tones of red, orange, and purple will create an overall blended effect that will go with medium tones of almost any other color. Adding a bright color to such a quilt, however, will make that color the focal point of the design.

Consider color values when you plan your quilt. Bright colors attract the eye immediately when they are placed next to softer ones. The best way to delineate a pattern is to juxtapose bright colors with neutral ones, or dark colors with light ones.

Since, traditionally, quilts make use of color and print combinations that you might consider bizarre by any other standards, you will find your color sensibility broadening as you begin planning quilt designs and working with cloth.

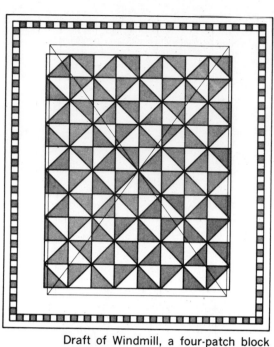

Draft of Windmill, a four-patch block design quilt with plain and patchwork borders. The quilt is designed so that its geometric block pattern will be centered on the bed. The bed size is marked by the rectangle in the draft; the center of the bed was determined by marking an X from corner to opposite corner of the rectangle.

THE DRAFT OR PLAN

A draft is a line drawing of a quilt. Making a draft will help you work out the proportions of your design and calculate the yardages you will need. It will also serve as a valuable reference guide for you as you sew.

Before you begin your draft, decide what size your quilt will be. Most quilts are made so that they cover the top of the bed and extend down 12 to 18 inches at the sides and foot. The table below lists the standard bed sizes, with corresponding quilt measurements:

STANDARD QUILT SIZES

	Beds		Quilts	
	Width	Length	Width	Length
Crib	28″	52″	37″	52″–56″
Twin	30″–39″	75″	66″	90″–96″
Full	54″	75″	80″	90″–96″
Queen	60″	80″	90″	96″–100″
King	76″	80″	104″	96″–100″

To draw the draft. Use 8½ by 11-inch graph paper with ten squares to the inch. If you are making an unusually long or wide quilt, tape two sheets of graph paper together, making sure that the lines on the paper match.

If your design does not have to be centered on the quilt (most designs don't), simply draw an outline of your quilt to scale and fit your design into the allotted area. If you want your quilt design to be centered on the bed (if you are making a medallion quilt, for example), or if you want the quilt blocks to be centered, begin by drawing an outline of your bed to scale in the center of the paper. With an X, mark the exact center of the bed. Next, draw an outline of the size of your quilt in the same scale around the outline of the bed. Then draw the design as you want it to appear when the quilt is placed on the bed. When you have plotted out your design to your satisfaction, you can experiment with the color plan by using colored pencils and either drawing over the draft on tracing paper or filling in the draft with the colors you choose.

Usually there is some take-up in a very puffy quilt after it has been quilted or tied. The Pre-stuffed Triangles quilt (page 61) was 1 inch shorter and narrower after it was sewn together. An extremely puffy quilt—the Irregular Design quilt described on page 68—was 8 inches narrower after quilting. If you are planning a draft for a puffy quilt, you may wish to take this factor into consideration.

The draft for the Pre-stuffed Triangles quilt is on page 61. An example of a draft for a center-design quilt is shown here.

PATTERNS

After you figure the sizes of your pattern pieces from your draft, draw each piece to actual size on paper. Then transfer the pattern of each piece to cardboard or sandpaper, using carbon paper. If you are making clear plastic patterns, place the plastic over the pattern piece, tape the pattern securely in place, and trace the outline of the pattern directly onto the plastic using a ball-point pen or a grease pencil. Add ¼ inch to the sides of the patterns for seam allowances. Before you proceed any further, cut several pieces out of cloth and sew them together along the ¼-inch seam allowances to test the accuracy of the patterns.

Materials. Patterns can be made out of cardboard, sandpaper, or plastic. Ordinary "shirt cardboard," the most readily available material, is entirely satisfactory. Sandpaper patterns, once very popular, can be cut from medium- to fine-grade sandpaper; they have the advantage of sticking slightly to the cloth as you mark it. Plastic is durable, and its transparency will allow you to see the design of the cloth as you mark patterns.

The other materials you will need for pattern making are: large pieces of paper for drawing blocks (newspaper is fine), a pencil, carbon paper, a ruler, scissors, and a compass for making circles. You may wish to smooth the edges of cardboard patterns with sandpaper.

Basic geometric shapes. Small squares, rectangles, and some triangles are simple enough to draw directly onto your pattern. To make a perfect equilateral triangle, a hexagon, or a six-pointed star, draw a circle with a compass, draw a second circle with a radius ¼ inch longer to allow for the ¼-inch seam allowance, and then mark off the circumference of the larger circle into six equal parts (the length of the radius) and connect the appropriate points (see the first diagram on the right). The diagram below it shows how to achieve the three-dimensional effect of cubes—baby blocks—by using different colors of cloth and basic geometric shapes.

Block designs. To make a square paper pattern to the actual size of one block (a complete design unit for a block quilt), first measure and mark equal lengths (the measure of one side of the block) from one corner of the paper along two adjacent sides. Fold the paper diagonally, at the two points marked, to form a triangle. Cut away the excess paper, using the two pre-cut edges as a guide (see diagram), open the triangle, and you will have a square.

This square is the basic design unit of hundreds of traditional quilt patterns. Subdividing the square by folding it in various ways will give you the guidelines for many of these designs and the patterns you will need to make them. Draw lines with a ruler and circles with a compass, using the folds or corners of the block as guides. Be sure to add a ¼-inch seam allowance to all pattern pieces.

The descriptions and diagrams on the following pages are based on different divisions of the square. Studying them will help you to understand how to reproduce most patchwork patterns. Once you have become familiar with the technique, you may wish to experiment with designs of your own.

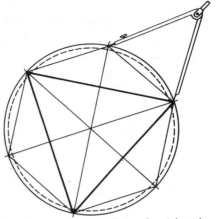

Drawing an equilateral triangle, hexagon, and six-pointed star

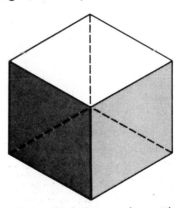

A hexagon shaded to make a "baby block." Placement of three patches according to tone will determine which part of the block stands out.

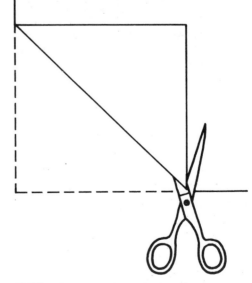

Cutting for a square paper pattern

PATCH PLANS FOR BLOCK DESIGNS

Four-patch. This is the most basic of all patch arrangements; it contains four squares of equal size, obtained by folding the block in half each way. The quarter-squares in the block may be divided into various kinds of triangles or other shapes. The four-patch is a strong, simple design and was traditionally used for two-color quilts. The top row illustrates the steps for folding and drawing the Windmill design; the bottom row, the Wild Goose Chase design.

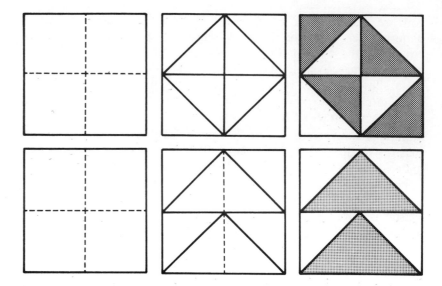

Sixteen-patch. After folding the square in half each way, fold it again into quarters to obtain sixteen squares. This plan is the basis for many designs; a great number of color variations are possible within each design. (Top) King's Crown design. (Bottom) Wind-blown Square.

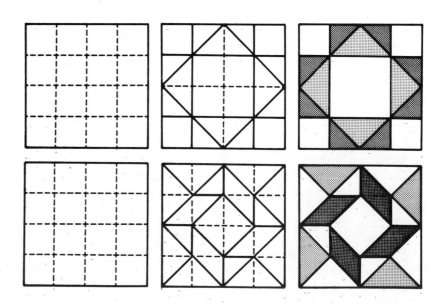

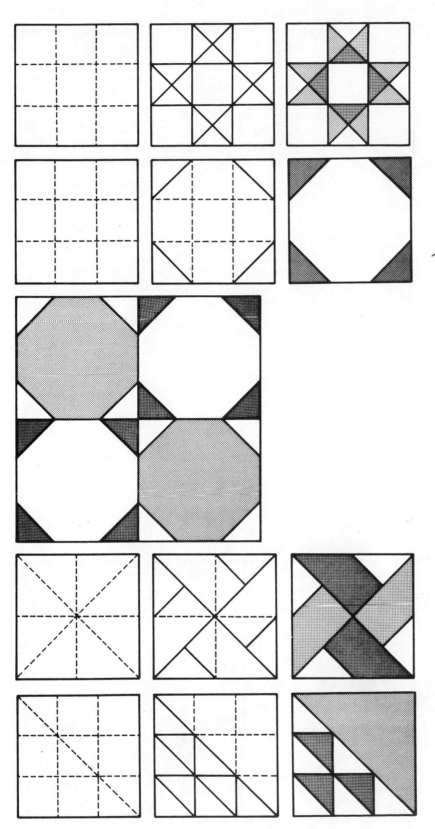

Nine-patch. Fold the square into three equal sections (see diagram). Then crease, unfold, and fold it into thirds the other way. The nine-patch pattern has always been a popular one, and is the starting point for many traditional designs. (Top) Variable Star. (Bottom) A Rob Peter to Pay Paul variation.

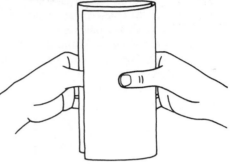

Folding for nine-patch

Patch plan plus diagonals. Make two diagonal folds from the corners of the block to form an X. Diagonal folds used in conjunction with horizontal or vertical folds are the basis for many star designs. (Top) Waterwheel. (Bottom) Birds in the Air.

Patch plan plus circles. A folded patch plan makes the center points for drawing circles. Any patch plan might be used. Also, any number and size circles could be drawn using a compass and folded points as the centers of the circles. For example, the diagram at right, below, shows four four-patch blocks. The radius of the circle is measured from the center of each block to the corner of each block; the circles overlap into the next block—hence the name of this design, Rob Peter to Pay Paul. The design shown at top is Steeplechase.

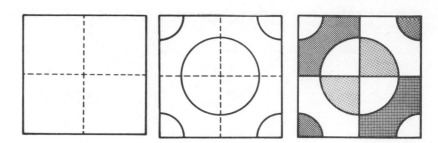

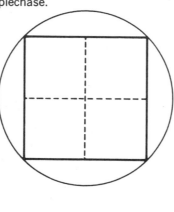

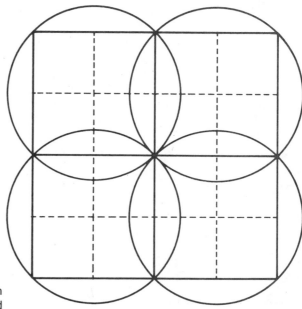

Detail, patchwork quilt, Rob Peter to Pay Paul, by Noreen Winkler. Photo by Ted Becker. The complete quilt is pictured on page 44.

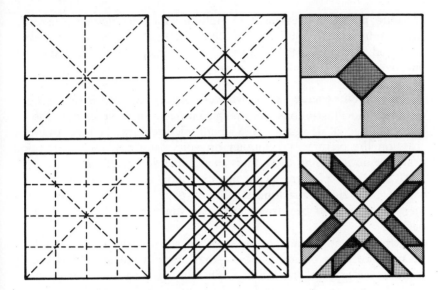

Patch plan plus crosses. Any patch plan might be used. The crosses may be horizontal and vertical, or diagonal. Parallel lines the desired width of the crosses are drawn equidistant from the center folds. The other features of the design rely on the other folds of the block. (Top) Bowtie. (Bottom) Mexican Cross.

Picture blocks. These are stylized patchwork pictures made up of combinations of squares. Flowers, trees, leaves, and baskets have been pictured in this way in the past. You can either fold the block many times, or rule out, for example, 1-inch squares, or use graph paper. (Top) Schoolhouse. (Bottom) Tulip.

Appliqué patterns. Designs for appliqué, such as flowers, leaves, fruits, animals, or abstract motifs, may be drawn freehand, traced, or copied. If you plan to use a shape many times, make your pattern out of plastic or cardboard, or else cut several patterns out of paper.

Paper cutouts (made like snowflakes), pictures of flowers from seed catalogs, and illustrations from magazines can all serve as patterns.

To enlarge a design from a small picture, draw an X and a cross on the picture and another on your pattern block. Then redraw the design using these lines as a guide (see diagram).

All appliqué patterns, with the exception of those to be sewn with a close zigzag machine stitch (see page 35), need a 3/16-inch seam allowance to be turned under as you sew the design to the backing.

Sections of appliqué that bend or curve, such as stems, should be made of cloth cut on the bias—that is, cloth cut at a 45 degree angle to the grain of the fabric. Quilt bindings and stems for patchwork flowers are also made from bias-cut cloth. Bias strips of cloth can be made easily by marking on both sides of a ruler and cutting.

Cutting without patterns. Cut large squares directly from cloth by using the method for cutting a paper square for a block design (see page 25). Dividing the cloth square in half diagonally will give you triangles, and cutting these in half will give you smaller triangles.

Cut stripes, lattice strips, stems, or borders without a pattern by measuring out the width of the strip on cloth, cutting for 4 inches, folding this section over for a guide, and cutting again. Continue folding and cutting until your strip is the desired length.

CLOTH ESTIMATES

In making an estimate of how much fabric you will require for your quilt, remember to include the top, borders and lattice strips, the backing, and the binding. Make your calculations at home with your pattern pieces, and base your estimate on a fabric width of 45 inches. (If you find later that the fabric you like is 36 inches wide, buy one and a quarter times as much as you would of 45-inch goods.)

The top. Using your colored draft, count each different shape patchwork piece or appliqué piece that is to be made of different-colored cloth (for example, 200 red triangles). Using a newspaper that is taped together to make a 45-inch width, or a piece of cloth that is 45 inches wide, move each of the pattern pieces across it, counting how many will fit in one row. Divide the number in one row into the total number of pieces of the pattern you need, and then multiply the result by the width of the rows of pieces to get the total yardage needed. For example: If 20 triangular pieces can be cut across a 45-inch width of cloth and you need 200 such triangles, first divide 200 by 20 to get the total number of rows needed—10. Ten is now multiplied by the depth of each row of

Enlarging an appliqué design from picture to pattern piece, using a cross and an X as guidelines.

(Above left) A brilliant red and green appliqué quilt of a typical nineteenth-century tulip design. The blocks were set diagonally, with cording between them, and the quilt was elaborately hand quilted. From the collection of Helen Montgomery. (Above right) Detail of a border tulip appliqué. Photos by Daniel Danneman.

triangles. If each row is 5 inches deep, the total yardage needed for the triangles is 50 inches of 45-inch wide cloth—about 1½ yards.

Borders and lattice strips. Calculate yardage for these in the same way as for patchwork. If you are using the same cloth for pattern pieces, cut the border pieces from the sides of the yardage first.

The back. The width of your quilt will determine what sort of fabric you use for the back. For example, the backing for a standard twin-size quilt, 66 inches wide, would best be made from two lengths of 36-inch wide material, with a seam running lengthwise down the middle. Seams may also run crosswise, or you can eliminate seams altogether by using a sheet, or 72-inch wide fabric if it is available. If you plan to bind your quilt by bringing the back over the top—see page 43—the back must be 2 to 4 inches larger, all around, than the top. If you plan to quilt on a frame, the back must be 4 inches longer on two opposite sides so that you can attach the quilt to the aprons of the frame. Usually the extra material is added to the longer sides so there will be less quilt to roll. But if the quilt is too long to fit the frame, add the extra material to the shorter sides. It will not be quilted (you can cut it off before binding), but you must add it in when calculating yardage requirements.

The binding. If you make your binding out of 1½-inch bias strips, you will need 1 yard of cloth 45 inches wide for an 80 by 96-inch quilt. You will need slightly less for a twin-size quilt and about 1½ yards for a queen-size quilt. If you make a self binding, using the overlap from the back, no extra binding cloth is necessary. (See the section on Binding, page 42.) Straight-cut binding should be estimated in the same way as borders and lattice strips (see above).

MARKING THE PATTERNS ON CLOTH

Mark squares and rectangles on the lengthwise or crosswise grain of the cloth. Mark diamond-shaped pieces with one edge on the grain. If possible, mark triangles with one side along the grain, but only if they look best cut this way. (Cut triangles and diamonds so that you will be able to sew a bias side to a straight side, to keep the pieces from stretching out of shape.) Pattern pieces may share a common line, whenever possible, to conserve fabric.

Place the pattern piece on the reverse side of the cloth and draw around it with a pencil, a ball-point pen, or, if the cloth is dark, a light dressmaker's pencil. When marking appliqué and asymmetrical pieces, turn the pattern piece wrong-side up so that you won't get a reverse piece. Mark carefully, and check the accuracy of your pattern by sewing a few pieces together before drawing them all.

CUTTING

Cut carefully, using your sharpest scissors. If you cut several layers of cloth at a time, use only simple shapes and lightweight fabric, or your pieces may not be completely accurate. Pin cut pieces of the same shapes together, or place them in envelopes, for safekeeping.

"Mirsini's Quilt" by Winifred Bendiner-Viani for Mirsini Whitten. An embroidered, center panel child's quilt with simple patchwork borders and self-binding.

Pinwheel block design wall hanging by Marilynn Fowler. Hand quilted, with lattice strips of patchwork squares. Note that the blocks themselves stand out distinctly; also note the repeated pattern shapes.

Clay's Choice, a hand-quilted block design wall hanging by Marilynn Fowler. Here the blocks blend together, although the pattern shape is repeated, and the totality of the design is emphasized by color placement.

Arranging "Airplane and Propeller" quilt blocks on the floor for color placement. These unique picture blocks by Barbara Elizabeth Chesterman are rectangular in shape and will be set diagonally.

Dresden Plate patchwork and appliqué sampler by Rosemarie Axton.

SEWING

The basic method for sewing a quilt is to make increasingly larger units out of smaller ones. For example, four triangles that make up a square block are first sewn together in pairs; the pairs are then sewn together to make up the block. When each block is completed, it is then sewn to other blocks to make a larger section of blocks. Then the sections are sewn together to make the quilt top.

Experimenting with the assembly of individual sections will show you the best way to proceed for your entire quilt.

Sewing patchwork by hand. Sew patchwork pieces by hand with a plain running stitch, using a single length of white or colored number 50 cotton thread, knotted at the end.

Pinning and basting are unnecessary, but be sure your sewing edges are even, and the right sides of the fabric are facing each other, before you start stitching. Stitch on the ¼-inch seam allowance as evenly as possible. Try to get three or four stitches on your needle before you pull the thread through, and aim for twelve stitches to the inch (six showing on each side). Sew over the last stitch three times to secure it before you cut the thread.

The top diagram on the facing page shows Dresden Plate patchwork pieces being sewn together. A completed Dresden Plate patchwork sampler appears on page 34.

Sewing patchwork by machine. Set your machine at ten stitches to the inch and stitch along the ¼-inch seam allowance. Stitch forward and backward at the beginning and end of each seam to secure the stitching.

Sewing appliqué by hand. Prepare for appliquéing by hand by turning the outside edge of each piece under to form a 3/16-inch hem. Notch the edges of curved pieces at ½-inch intervals and then turn them under. Crease the hems down with your fingers, or baste them down, keeping the knot on top of the pieces so the basting can be pulled out easily. (Basting and pressing are not absolutely necessary—you can turn edges under as you sew.)

The best stitch to use in sewing appliqué by hand is the whip stitch (see the bottom diagram), the same type of stitch commonly used in hemming. The thread you use should match the appliqué pieces, not the background fabric. Pin the appliqué pieces to the background. Begin sewing by catching the knot of the thread under the edge of the piece. Then make a small stitch through the background fabric, and come up through the appliqué edge again. Starting your stitches through the background material just under each appliqué piece and keeping them quite small will help you to have even edges and stitches that are almost invisible.

Sewing appliqué by machine. Using a sewing machine for appliqué creates a very different effect from hand sewing. A machine zigzag stitch will outline each piece in a highly visible fashion. Machine sewing is durable, and looks very good with modern designs. If you use fairly close machine stitching, it is not necessary to turn the edges of your pieces under.

IRONING

You should iron when all your blocks have been completed, just before setting them. First iron on the wrong side, pressing the seams closed and to one side. Then iron the block on the right side to make sure the surface is flat. Iron again once the quilt is set, to press the new seams.

SETTING

Setting is the process of sewing blocks or strips together, and it is done when all the top sections of the quilt are complete.

Place all your blocks or sections on a flat surface and check the arrangement to make sure that you like it. Now is the time to see that the balance of colors is right and that the proportion of lattice or border strips to the quilt pattern is perfect. This step is rather like that of an artist's stepping away to look at his canvas.

When you are satisfied with your arrangement, decide which quilting method you will use. (See the section on Quilting, page 36.)

If you decide that your quilt will be quilted or tied in one piece, sew the blocks together into larger sections, and then into strips. This will leave you with several very large sections, which you can

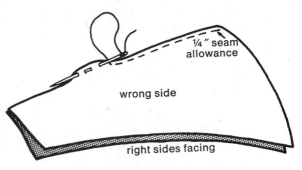

Sewing patchwork pieces by hand

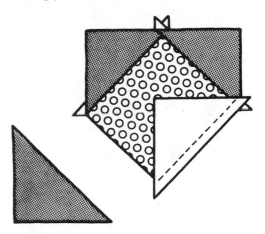

Sewing triangle- and square-shaped patchwork pieces. When you attach triangles to squares, the corner points of the triangles will extend as shown in the diagram. Be very careful when you attach the next blocks not to cut off the corners of the square.

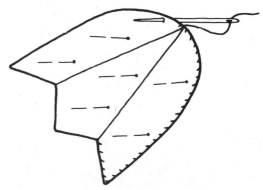

Sewing appliqué pieces by hand using the whip stitch. Fold a hem under as you go, stitching the edge with close, small stitches.

then sew together by hand or machine. Many quiltmakers prefer to sew the long seams connecting the larger sections of their quilts by machine, even if they have sewn the blocks by hand, because machine stitching is faster and stronger.

Without basting, pin and sew a standard ¼-inch seam. Start from the center and sew to one edge. Then go back to the center and sew to the other edge (see diagram **h** on page 51). Starting at the center helps to make seam junctions accurate; but in any case, proceed slowly, and stop to correct any junction of blocks that does not meet. (Slight imperfections in the seam junctions are common, and not very noticeable after the quilt is finished.) Before you decrease or enlarge an intersecting seam, check to see how it will affect the next junction and the general flatness of the quilt.

Press the seams to one side, and then iron the entire quilt, both the back and the front.

If you decide to quilt or tie your quilt in sections rather than in one piece, proceed according to the directions on page 41.

QUILTING

The purpose of quilting. Quilting is the basic method of connecting the top, filling, and back of a quilt by sewing them together, usually using small, even stitches in a decorative design. Quilting creates another element in the design, outlining and raising portions of the pattern, and giving emphasis and dimension to certain sections. The quilting method you choose will affect the entire design of your quilt. For this reason, you should consider the amount of space in your home that you can devote to quilting, the amount of time you can spend on it, and the thickness of the filling you plan to use before you choose the quilting method that is most suitable for you. Quilting can be done by hand on a quilting frame, on a hoop, or with the quilt lying on a table—or you can use a sewing machine (see page 42). Quilting by sections is described on page 41. Read this entire section thoroughly before deciding on the method you will use for your particular project.

Quilting designs. The two most common methods of quilting are quilting in straight lines—crosses, triangles, diamonds, or squares—and outline quilting—that is, stitching on the inside or outside of the design. Outline quilting may cover the entire top, or accentuate only certain sections of the design. Another way of quilting is to sew scallops, waves, swirls, or chainlike rows of stitches. A fourth, less popular method of quilting is elaborate pictorial quilting that creates a complete design of its own. While the first three methods of quilting can often be done by eye, the last type needs to be marked onto the quilt top.

Most modern quilts are not quilted as heavily or as elaborately as those done in the past—it isn't necessary anymore. Old-fashioned cotton batting comes apart unless it is quilted quite closely, but quilts filled with dacron that have rows of quilting up to 12 inches apart will withstand years of washing and use without coming apart inside, if washed by hand.

The back of the Hummingbird block by Pat Thompson, from the appliqué presentation quilt shown on page 76, illustrates outline quilting.

A traditional Sunbonnet Baby quilt and details by Annabel Pico. Patchwork triangle blocks alternate with pictorial appliqué blocks enriched with embroidery and rickrack.

"Jay's Quilt," designed, printed, and quilted by Joanne Brandford. The blocks are of silk-screen-printed cotton cloth, appliquéd and reverse appliquéd, and pieced together by machine. The binding is of the same silk-screen cloth.

Marking for quilting. If you wish to do pictorial quilting, or to mark lines for quilting, draw the design onto your quilt with a pencil or a dressmaker's pencil, using a ruler to mark straight lines and a compass or saucer for circles. Pencil will begin to wear off as you sew, and any remaining marks will disappear in the first washing of the quilt. You can also scratch the quilt surface lightly with your needle, as you sew, to mark a line.

Quilting patterns. If you'd like to use an elaborate quilting design, but would rather not make up your own, you can buy perforated quilting patterns from quilting pattern suppliers. These designs are transferred to the quilt by marking through the perforations with pencil or chalk. You can also make your own jigsawlike cardboard patterns and trace around them.

Quilting by hand. While quilting may be unlike any sewing you have done before, it is basically very easy, and you will probably catch on quickly.

Medium-length, flexible number 8, 7, or 6 sharps or millinery needles are preferred for quilting because they are easy to manipulate. Experiment, though, to see if you like shorter or longer needles better. White is the traditional color for quilting thread, but either white or colored number 50 cotton thread is acceptable. Special silicone-coated thread that will not tangle or knot is also available.

Whether you are using a hoop, a quilting frame, or working on a table, the basic sewing technique is the same. Always begin quilting in the center of the quilt. Make the smallest knot possible at the end of a short single length of thread (an arm's length—about 30 inches), and tug the thread through the back into the filling from underneath. Or start from underneath without a knot, hold onto the end of the thread with one hand, and tack the first stitch three times over to secure the thread.

The quilting stitch looks like a running stitch. Usually, though, only one stitch can be done at a time—that is, down and back up—when you are quilting on a frame or a hoop. The needle works like a seesaw. Hold your needle at a 45 degree angle to the quilt and sew down through all the layers of the quilt. Your hand under the quilt will feel the point of the needle as you sew through; push the cloth slightly up and around the needle. Weight the eye end of the needle with your middle fingers as you sew back up, for leverage. Keep the surface of the quilt slightly looser than drum-tight when you quilt on a frame or a hoop. Take short, neat stitches—about eight to an inch—and stitch along quickly, getting a rhythm going. Keep the stitches as even as possible. Always leave some ease in the thread to avoid puckers, and secure the thread by tacking the last stitch three times over.

Plan the path of your sewing and be sure the needle travels through the filling to hold it in place when there are spaces between quilted areas. Use a thimble, or tape, or a rubber finger guard to protect your fingers, and run dressmaker's beeswax over the thread if it tangles—or run the thread over a candle.

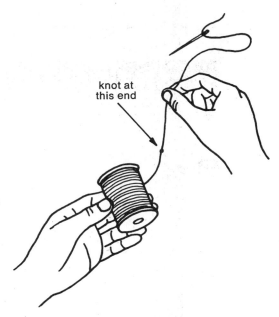

knot at this end

To avoid tangles, thread needle with the end by which you pull the thread off the spool. Knot where thread is cut from the spool.

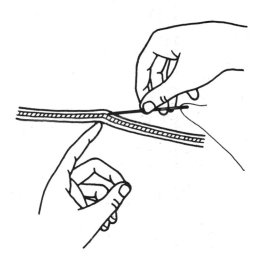

The position of the hands for the quilting stitch

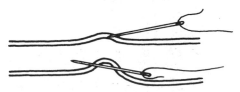

The see-saw motion of the needle as one quilting stitch is sewn

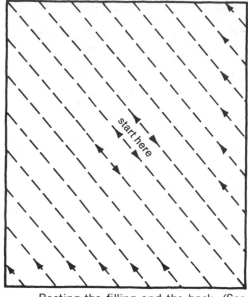

start here

Basting the filling and the back. (See page 41 for directions.)

The quilting frame. There are many ways to quilt, but using a frame is the most functional method for doing unrestrained stitching. The quilt is held taut, and both hands are free for sewing.

The long sides of the frame are called rolling bars. The quilt is attached to aprons the length of a standard-size quilt on these bars, and, as the quilt is stitched, finished portions are rolled around the bars and out of the way. (To calculate the yardage required for attaching the back of your quilt to a frame, see page 32.)

It is possible to dismantle the quilting frame when it is not being used, but when it is in use, the frame will take up a good deal of room. If you have enough space, and want to use a frame, you can buy one ready-made or you can put one together yourself (see diagram below). To construct your own, cut 1 by 3's (for the rollers) 12 inches longer than your quilt; attach aprons. Make the 1 by 2 side rails 3 feet long. Hold these boards together with C clamps. To use, rest the frame between two tables or chairs.

The Around the World quilt was quilted on a frame. Each step of this project is illustrated, beginning on page 47.

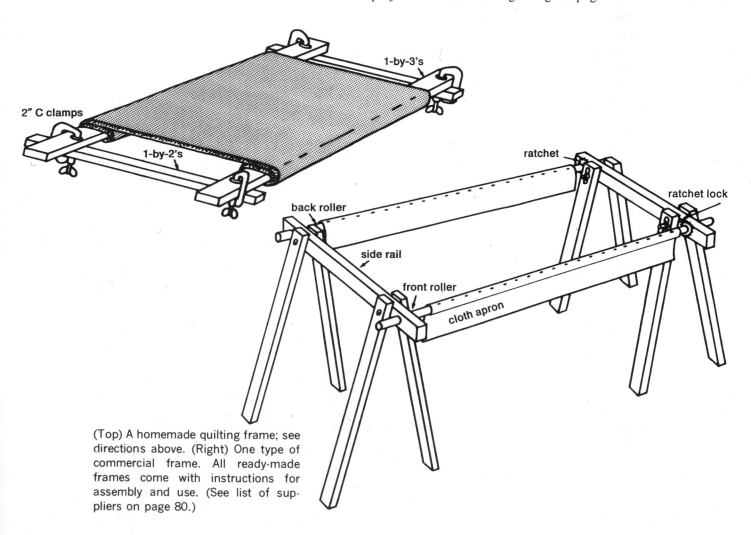

1-by-3's

2" C clamps

1-by-2's

ratchet

ratchet lock

back roller

side rail

front roller

cloth apron

(Top) A homemade quilting frame; see directions above. (Right) One type of commercial frame. All ready-made frames come with instructions for assembly and use. (See list of suppliers on page 80.)

QUILTING BY SECTIONS

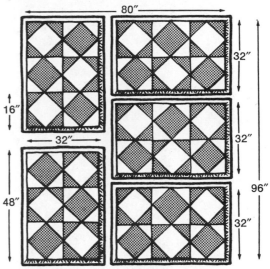

a. Blocks set and stacked

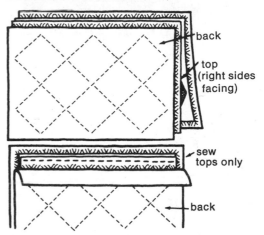

b. Attaching the blocks

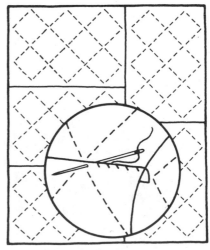

c. Finishing the back seams

Basting the layers of a quilt together is not absolutely necessary if you use a frame (although it is helpful if the quilting is to be done by a group). However, you will need basting to hold the layers of the quilt together if you use any other method of quilting.

There are two steps in basting. First, open up the filling and place it flat on the floor or on a table. Place the back on top, right side out. Pin, and baste as illustrated on page 40. Next, turn these two layers over and place the top over the filling, even the edges, and pin and baste again, in the *opposite* diagonal direction, to make a grid of secure basting.

The same basting technique is used for both steps. First, baste three center rows, approximately 9 inches apart. Begin at the middle of each row, and using ¾-inch-long stitches, baste diagonally to one edge. Then go back to the center and baste to the opposite edge. The rest of the diagonal rows may be basted directly from one side of the quilt to the other. (If the quilting, too, will be done in diagonal rows, baste slightly to one side of where you want the quilting to be.)

Quilting with a hoop. A quilting hoop or a large embroidery hoop has the advantages of being portable, easy to handle, inexpensive, and efficient. Large embroidery hoops (a good size is 18 by 27 inches) can be found in most needlework stores or in the sewing departments of large department stores. They can also be ordered by mail (see the list of suppliers on page 80).

If you use a hoop, baste your quilt first, leaving the edges open. Place the quilting hoop in the center of your quilt and adjust the screws on the side of the hoop to hold the quilt as taut as you'd like it to be. Usually the outside edges are quilted without the hoop.

Quilting by sections. With this efficient, uncomplicated method, the quilt is assembled, or set, after, and not before, it is quilted. Units or sections of blocks of up to one-fourth of the quilt are quilted separately, and then joined together, according to the following method (letters refer to diagrams):

a. First, set blocks into sections. (The diagram shows how a standard quilt, 80 by 96 inches, might be divided. Each section in this example is 32 by 48 inches, which is an easy size to quilt without a hoop or frame.) Cut the back for each section 2 inches larger all around than the top (for joining the sections later); cut the filling the same size as the top. Stack, baste, and quilt each section to within ¼ inch of the edge of the top. (Be sure to leave these seam allowances unquilted.)

b. After all sections have been quilted, connect them as follows: One by one, place the tops of the quilted sections with their right sides together and sew the tops together with a running stitch, either by hand or machine. Leave the back seams open.

c. Once the entire quilt top is set, press it flat, turn the quilt to the back, and finish the back seams by overlapping one back edge over the next. Crease a hem with your fingers on each overlapping edge and whip stitch it down. Bind the quilt (see Binding, page 42).

Detail of Roman Stripe patchwork quilt by Leila Shomer, quilted with cross-stitch embroidery.

Quilting by sewing machine. Quilting by machine is not as easy as it might seem; maneuvering a large, bulky quilt around under the arm of a sewing machine while keeping the quilting even and smooth can be difficult indeed.

If you plan to quilt by machine, therefore, you must baste your quilt quite closely, and be sure that the filling you use is not too thick. Dacron filling should be no more than ¼-inch thick. A sheet of cotton flannel would be even easier to handle.

Set your machine for eight stitches to the inch and sew in straight lines (horizontal, vertical, or diagonal) from one edge to the other. Sew the center rows of quilting first—for example, from corner to opposite corner if you are doing diagonal quilting. Check each line of stitching as you complete it to make sure there are no puckers on the back.

The amount of space you leave open at the edge of the quilt depends on how you decide to bind it. (See Binding, below.) An interesting effect is achieved by quilting to within a foot of the edge and then quilting around the perimeter of the quilt to make a border.

Other methods of assembling a quilt. Four additional methods are described in connection with special projects. Tying—a simple way to join the top, filling, and back of a quilt by tying them together at regular intervals with short lengths of cotton or wool yarn—is described for the Random-color Squares quilt on page 58. The other methods are: stuffing from an open end (Irregular Design quilt, page 68); pre-stuffing (Pre-stuffed Triangles quilt, page 61); and trapunto (Trapunto quilt, page 74).

BINDING

The final step in making a quilt is binding off the edges. There are several ways to do this, and each has certain advantages. Remember that if you have quilted on a frame, there will be an extra 4 inches of material on two opposite sides of the back of the quilt (where it was attached to the frame).

Self binding. Turning in the edges of the top and back of a quilt so that they meet is a traditional, easy, and efficient method of binding. It is also flat and inconspicuous, and does not conflict with the quilt's design.

If you decide to bind your quilt in this way, do not quilt beyond ½ inch from the edges. Then even the top and the back edges and trim the filling so that it is ¼-inch shorter than the edges of the quilt. Turn the raw edges of the top and back under ¼ inch and crease the hems with your fingers. Pin the edges together. Sew them with an ordinary whip stitch (see page 35) or a slip stitch. The slip stitch makes an invisible finish: Pull the knot to the inside of the top hem, stitch through the hem to the back hem, take a stitch, then go diagonally across and stitch through the top hem, then back again, and so on. (You never go through the outside edge of the top or the back.)

The Around the World quilt on page 48 has a self binding.

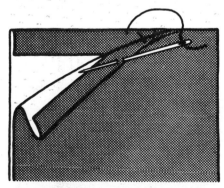

Slip stitch. Note that the stitches don't go through the outside edge, making an invisible finish.

The back as binding. This is another kind of self binding. You may turn the edges of the back of your quilt over the edges of the top to make a binding. If you wish to do this, make sure the back of your quilt is 2 to 4 inches larger all around than the top. Trim the top and the filling so that their edges are flush, or so that the filling extends a bit to fill the binding, and then fold the back edges over the top and whip stitch them down, turning a hem under as you sew. Whip stitch to within ¼ inch of the corners, and then fold the fabric to make mitered corners and stitch (see the diagram on the right).

To bind the edges by turning your quilt inside out, see the directions for stuffing from an open end on page 68.

Strip bindings: When a strip binding is to be added to the edge of a quilt, quilting may extend completely to the edges. A bias binding is used if the corners of the quilt are rounded because it will bend neatly around the curve. A straight binding, made of strips cut up and down or across the cloth, will have to have squared or mitered corners. Either type of strip is applied to the sides of the quilt in the same way—only the corners are handled differently.

BACK AS BINDING

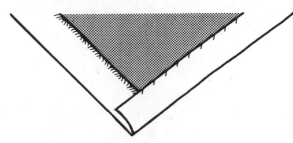

a. One side of back folded over top and whip stitched down

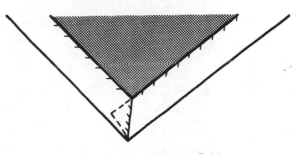

b. Making a mitered corner. Fold second corner under to make a 45 degree angle, and whip stitch down.

Weather Vane patchwork quilt by Marilynn Fowler. The block design radiates from the center; the quilt is hand quilted and has straight-cut borders and binding, with squared corners (see page 45).

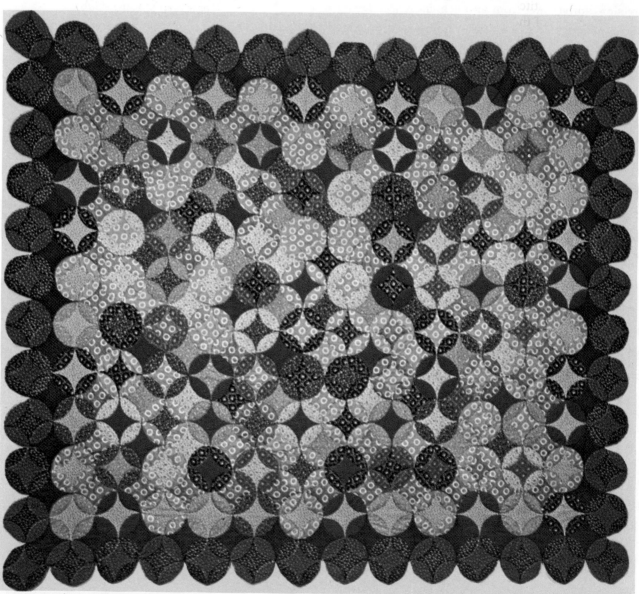

Rob Peter to Pay Paul patchwork quilt by Noreen Winkler. Although the design is a patch-plan block design, the pieces were cut and sewn whole, without block seams.

Bias binding. Cut the corners of the quilt so that they have a gentle curve. Trim the edges of the quilt with the filling protruding slightly so it will fill the binding. A commercial bias tape labeled "wide" can be used, or you can make your own. Bias binding is made of cloth cut on the bias—that is, cloth cut at a 45 degree angle to the grain of the fabric. To make your own, cut bias strips of cloth, 1¼ to 3 inches wide, using a ruler or a cardboard strip as a guide. (A yard of cloth will make enough 1½-inch strips to bind an 80 by 96-inch quilt.)

Sew the strips together with the seam on the straight grain, trim if necessary, and iron the seams open (see top diagram). Then machine or hand stitch the binding to the back edge of the quilt with the right sides of the binding and the quilt together. Start at the middle of one side. Turn the beginning end of the strip under ¼ inch. Make sure that the edge of the strip is flush with the raw edge of the back, and machine or hand stitch completely around the outside of the quilt, 3/16 inch from the edge. Bend the strip around the corners as you sew. Let the raw edge at the end of the strip overlap the folded edge at the beginning—it will be covered when the binding is folded up over the top.

Fold the binding away from the quilt and press along the seam. Turn the quilt right side up (see second diagram) and fold the binding over the top edge. Crease a hem with your fingers (commercial binding has a ready-made fold) and whip stitch the binding, turning a hem as you go.

Straight-cut binding, squared corners. (The corners are generally finished so the opposite sides match, as shown in diagram **a.**) Cut 1¼- to 1½-inch wide strips, and sew them together. The strips can all be one kind of cloth, or pieced together from different kinds of cloth —a kind of patchwork binding. Iron the seams open. Sew the binding to the top and bottom edges of the quilt first. Place the right sides of the binding and the back of the quilt together, with the edge of the binding even with the edge of the quilt. Sew from corner to corner, stop, cut the thread, and cut the binding off even with the quilt. Press the back of the quilt, opening the binding, and turn the quilt right side up. Fold the binding over the top edge and the bottom edge, crease a hem with your fingers, and whip stitch the binding down (see diagram **b**).

Sew the side binding in the same way, leaving ½ inch of binding extending beyond the edge of the quilt at both the top and the bottom. Press the binding open, and then turn the ½-inch extension over the binding (see diagram **c**). Fold the binding over, making a squared corner, and whip stitch down.

To make a mitered corner, sew the binding to the top and bottom edges of the quilt in the same way as for squared corners. Sew the side bindings with a ¼-inch extension at both the top and bottom. Fold and tuck the extensions under and even with the top and bottom edges of the quilt. Fold the binding over the top, and crease the corners at a 45 degree angle. Whip stitch the corners and the hem.

BIAS BINDING

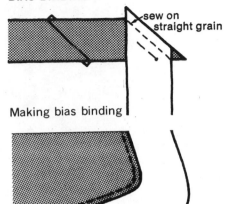

sew on straight grain

Making bias binding

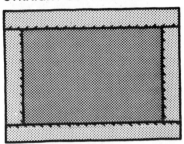

Attaching bias binding

STRAIGHT-CUT BINDING

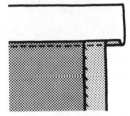

a. The bound quilt

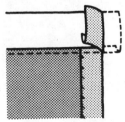

b. One side of binding whip stitched down

c. Fold extension up and binding over, making a squared corner.

Projects

Quilts and quilt designs are as numerous and unique as the people who make them. The step-by-step projects that follow suggest what you can do with quiltmaking once you have learned the basic techniques. Throughout the book you will also find pictured many examples of historical and contemporary quilts. They are here not only to show you what can be accomplished, but also to inspire you to experiment with color and cloth, and create your own designs. The quilt you make will really be your own—one that only you could have made.

Appliqué Sampler

Sampler Size: 13½″ × 13½″

Content

Top: ½ yd. muslin; ¼ yd. each cotton print for the appliqués
  Note: The polka-dot hearts may be pieced together from scraps
Filling: ½ yd. cotton flannel or one 13½″ square of dacron polyester fiberfill
Back: ½ yd. cotton

Sewing: By hand

Quilting: By hand on a small embroidery hoop

Binding: Self-bound

Making a sampler is an excellent way to practice the techniques of quiltmaking before you embark on a large project. The sampler pictured here is an original design of appliqué hearts on muslin. The quilting was marked in pencil before stitching, and follows the outline of the hearts.

If you would like to try making an appliqué sampler like this one, follow the general appliqué directions given on page 35. If you wish to try a patchwork sampler, follow the patchwork directions on page 34.

The sampler here is self-bound: The edges of the back are turned over the top, making a framelike border (this method is described on page 43). The top is 13 inches square before binding; the filling, 13½ inches square; and the back, 16 inches square. Once the ¾-inch back binding is turned over the top, the overall measurement of the sampler is 13½ by 13½ inches.

Appliqué Heart sampler. Red-and-white and pink-and-orange polka-dot hearts on unbleached muslin top, with an orange border.

Around the World Quilt

Quilt Size: 88″ × 96″ (4″ squares)

Content

Top: 8 yds. 45″ cotton and cotton blends—different colors in ¼-yd. pieces (5 yds. would be sufficient if all one kind of cloth is used); 5 yds. unbleached permanent-press muslin

Filling: 88″ × 96″ piece of dacron polyester fiberfill

Back: One queen-size permanent-press muslin sheet. *Note:* The back must be cut 4″ longer on the top and the bottom edges than the top and filling, so that it can be attached to the apron of the quilting frame.

Sewing: By hand and machine

Quilting: Hand quilted on a frame

Binding: Self-bound

The Around the World design is a classic one—the quilt is attractive, easy to assemble, and makes use of all the traditional quiltmaking techniques. If you read through these directions carefully, you will become well acquainted with these techniques and can apply them to whatever projects you choose. Around the World, a four-patch block design, is one of a great number of Drunkard's Path variations. The method for making the patterns for all the Drunkard's Path designs, including Around the World, is the same. Though all of these designs look complicated, they are composed of only two pattern pieces—a quarter circle and a curved L piece—the components of each patch of this four-patch design. The arrangement of the patches, which can be done in any number of different ways, is what makes the design look complicated. Each Drunkard's Path variation pictured here is made of a combination of calico prints and unbleached muslin.

Some Drunkard's Path designs. Left row, top to bottom: Baby Bunting, Around the World variation, Mill Wheel. Right row, top to bottom: Falling Timbers, Fool's Puzzle, Solomon's Puzzle.

STEPS FOR AROUND THE WORLD QUILT

(letters refer to photos and diagrams)

a. The draft. Make rough sketches until you have the plan for the quilt fairly well worked out. Then make the draft according to the directions given on page 24. In this particular quilt the size of the four-patch block is 8 by 8 inches; each patch is therefore 4 by 4 inches. The pattern for a design of repeated blocks is begun in the center of the graph paper and worked outward. The notes along the left-hand side of the draft pictured here indicate the number of pieces of each shape needed for each horizontal row of patches—that is, the number of plain muslin quarter-circles, of colored quarter-circles, of plain muslin L pieces, and of colored L pieces.

b. Paper and cardboard patterns. To make the paper pattern, fold an 8-inch-square piece of paper into quarters to make four 4-inch squares. Use the center point to draw a circle with a compass. The circle used here (see diagram **b** on page 49) occupies about two-thirds of the square, but the size of the circle is a matter of personal taste, and you can make it larger or smaller if you wish. To

a. The draft

Around the World patchwork quilt. Step-by-step instructions for making this classic block design quilt begin on page 47.

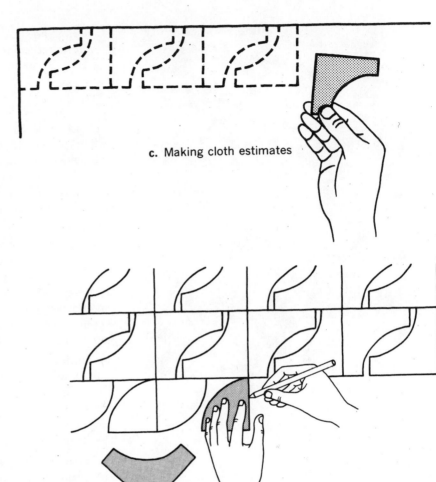

c. Making cloth estimates

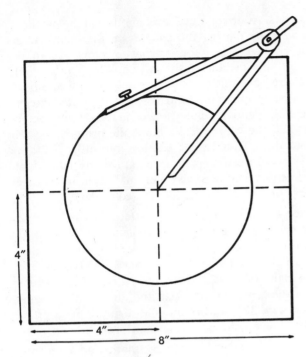

b. Making a paper pattern

d. Marking the pattern pieces

make the cardboard patterns, cut out and transfer one quarter-circle piece and the corresponding curved L piece to cardboard using carbon paper. Add ¼ inch to each side of the cardboard patterns for seam allowance. Cut and sew a pair of pieces to test them for accuracy (see step **e**). These patterns can be used for any of the Drunkard's Path variations shown on page 47.

c. Cloth estimates. Use the method outlined on page 30 for estimating the yardage needed for the plain muslin. For the colored pieces, an exact estimate cannot be made because scraps of material are used. (Eight yards of ¼-yard pieces of printed cotton were used to make this quilt.)

d. Marking and cutting. Outline the pattern pieces on the reverse side of the cloth with a ball-point pen. Place the straight sides of the patterns along the grain of the cloth. Cut all the muslin pieces and about half the colored pieces. (You will cut the rest of the colored pieces once you have sewn half the patches and have placed them out on the floor to see the effect—see step **f**, page 50.)

e. Sewing the patches. Place the quarter circles and the L shapes together, right sides facing. Sew by hand along the ¼-inch seam allowance, easing the circles around the L pieces as you sew. End each seam by going over the last stitch three times.

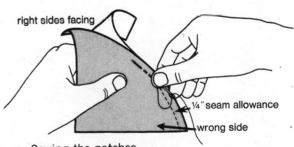

right sides facing

¼" seam allowance

wrong side

e. Sewing the patches

f. Arranging the patches

g. Sewing the sections

f. Arranging the patches. After you have sewn about half the patches, see how the colors work by placing the patches on the floor. Make notes and cut more colored pieces for whichever colors you think you need. Look at the illustration of the Around the World quilt on page 48. There are medallions of colors in various families: pinks, purples, browns, blacks, tans, and roses. The center circles are all reds. The colors blend to make a secondary design theme while the red circles and the white muslin make the primary theme. The effect is supposed to look rather careless but it is actually completely planned. If you need to pick up or move any individual patch, insert a piece of paper in its place. You may need to arrange and rearrange several times before you like the color design.

g. Sewing the sections. Once you have completed the patches, and you know how you want them arranged, sew them into sections of sixteen patches each. (All the sections but one will be four patches wide; that section will be six patches wide.) Sew the patches first into rows, then into pairs of rows, and so on. All the circle seams should face out from the center of the circle and all the other seams should face the same way. The sewing may be done by hand or by machine. Iron the sections on the back and then press the top.

h. Setting. Set the sections by twos, then by fours, and then into long rows. Make five long rows. Sew the rows into pairs and add the fifth row to one of these pairs. Last, connect these two final rows. When setting the long rows, sew each seam that runs the length of the quilt from the middle of the row to one edge. Then sew from the middle to the other edge. Iron the completed top.

i. Attaching the back to the frame. This quilt will be attached to the frame at the top and the bottom, so the top and the bottom edges of the back must be cut 4 inches longer than the edges of the quilt top so that they can be attached to the apron. To attach the back, first fold it in half and mark the center with pins at both sides. Next, center the back on the apron of the frame and then pin and sew one end securely in place (see diagram). Roll the back onto this roller and pin and sew the other end. Make sure that the back is centered and even on the frame. If you choose to baste your quilt, you can attach it to the frame using the same method.

j. Attaching the filling and the top. Mark the center of the filling and the center of the top with pins. Then place the filling over the frame and match these center pins with the center pins on the back. The filling will drape over both sides of the frame. Next, center the top and pin all three layers horizontally across the middle of the quilt. Make sure all the pins are horizontal, also, so they will roll easily with the quilt. Unroll one side of the back. Then temporarily roll all three layers onto this roller. Do not pin first. (It is a good idea to have someone to help you roll.) This makes it possible to pin the other side. Check that the quilt is even at the sides. Pin the edges of the filling and the top to the back with a row of horizontal pins placed every 4 inches. Do not pin these layers through the apron. Roll the quilt to the opposite side and pin this end the same way. Roll back to the first side and re-pin if necessary. Roll to the middle and begin quilting.

k. Quilting and binding. Smooth the back and the top of the quilt and pin together the three layers of the area you are about to quilt. Once this area is quilted, remove the pins and pin another area. You might need to pin strips of muslin to the sides of the quilt and around the frame to keep the sides taut. Remove and re-pin these also as you roll the quilt. As you quilt, adjust the side ratchets so that the surface of the quilt is firm, but not taut. The quilting for the Around the World quilt is an example of outline quilting—the stitches travel around the white medallions and center circles. The quilting makes the white areas slightly raised. The actual quilting stitch is described in detail on page 39. As you quilt toward the ends of the quilt, the rows of pins that attach the top and filling may have to be moved slightly one way or the other and re-pinned if there are puckers. Remove the quilt from the frame when the quilting is complete. Cut all the edges even, turn the top and back edges under, and bind by whip stitching them together (see page 35).

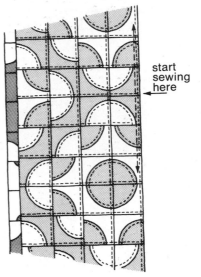

start sewing here

h. Setting the sections

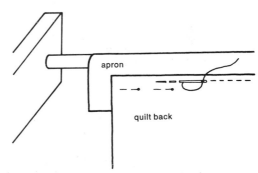

apron

quilt back

i. Attaching the back to the frame

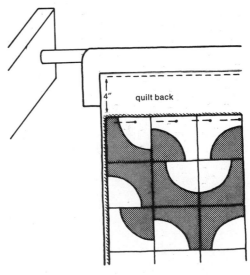

4"   quilt back

j. Attaching the filling and the top

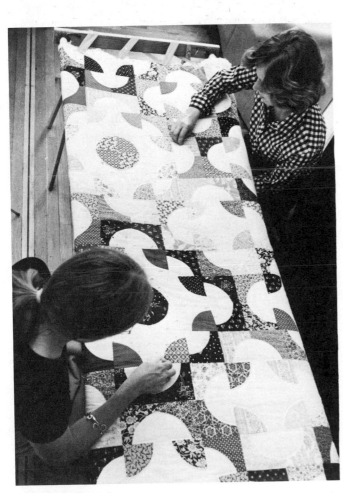

k. Quilting on a frame

Log Cabin Pocketbook

Pocketbook Size: 14″ × 14″ (the strap is 30″ long)

Content

Front, Back, and Strap: An assortment of cotton and cotton blends (prints and solids)

Lining and Strap Facing: ½ yd. muslin

Sewing: By machine

Collections of old quilts usually contain several variations of the ever-popular Log Cabin motif. This attractive block design depends upon the juxtaposition of darker or brighter shades of cloth with lighter shades. The color range generally moves from light logs in the center of each block to darker ones at the edge of the block.

A design with matching logs on opposite sides of the middle square, as illustrated on page 1, is called Courthouse Steps. All the other Log Cabin design variations have blocks with darker and lighter logs at adjacent corners. When blocks are set together with the logs forming diagonal rows, the design is called Straight Furrow. If the corners are turned to make light and dark diamonds that increase in size, the pattern is called Barn Raising (see the example on page 2). The crosslike design used for the tablecloth shown on page 54 is called Dark and Light.

Small block-design projects like the pocketbook here and the tablecloth on page 54 are excellent beginning projects; they also make nice gifts. The same pattern pieces are used to make the blocks for both projects. The size of the block as well as the width and number of logs that make up the block is up to you. (However, since it is difficult to work with odd fractions, it is advisable to make the logs 1, 1½, or 2 inches wide.)

This block design can be expanded into a quilt by simply making and connecting more blocks. (If you decide to make a quilt, set the blocks in rows and then connect the rows. Log Cabin quilts are traditionally tied rather than quilted.)

To make the pocketbook pictured on the facing page, you will need two blocks—one for the front of the purse and one for the back.

Patterns. This design starts from a central square that acts as a sort of bull's-eye. The square is in an accent color and is not part of the dark and light color progression of the logs. This block design is shown on page 55. (A diagram showing another traditional method of arranging the logs is also illustrated on page 55.)

The block used for this pocketbook is 14 inches square and the width of each log is 2 inches. Draw a 14-inch square and then rule out 2-inch squares as guides for the width of your logs. The four pattern pieces needed are outlined in the draft to the left. (Logs can be added or subtracted easily using this method.) When the draft is finished, measure each log and redraw the patterns on cardboard, being sure to add a ¼-inch seam allowance on each side.

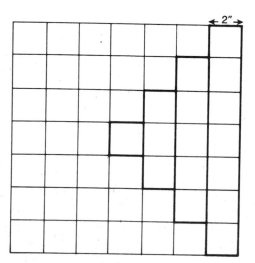

Pattern pieces ("logs") for Log Cabin block design. A 14-inch square is ruled out in 2-inch squares, and the four pattern pieces drawn as illustrated.

(Left) Log Cabin patchwork pocketbook. (Above) Georgetown Circle patchwork pillow of tie silk; see page 56. (Below) Patchwork block design pillows by Marilynn Fowler in the following patterns, from left to right: Steeplechase, King's Crown, Clay's Choice, Weather Vane, Eight-pointed Star, Roman Stripe, Columns. Photo by Bill Wagner. Directions for block designs are given on page 25; directions for making pillows are on page 57.

The Log Cabin patchwork tablecloth in the Dark and Light pattern (see facing page for instructions).

Sewing and setting. Sew the block from the center outwards. First, sew the three center squares together. Then add two logs to the sides of these squares. Add the next two logs to the top and bottom, and so on. When the block is completed, turn it to the back, and iron the seams closed facing the edges of the block. Make a second block for the back of the purse.

Iron both Log Cabin blocks. Place the right sides of the blocks together and sew around three sides, leaving the top open. Turn the blocks right side out.

Lining. Cut two 14½-inch squares of muslin for the lining and sew around three sides, leaving the top open. Drop the lining into the bag; turn both the outside edge and the lining edge in, and whip stitch or slip stitch around the top of the bag.

The strap is made of strips of squares and is 30 inches long—shoulder length. Use the center square from the Log Cabin block as a pattern. First, sew two long strips of squares. Iron. Using one strip for a pattern, cut a lining strip for reinforcement. Place the right sides of the strap together with the lining on top. Sew completely around the strap, leaving one end open. Using the eraser end of a pencil, push from the seamed end of the strap through to the open end so that the strap turns right side out. Turn the open ends under and whip stitch them closed. Iron the strap. Sew the strap just inside the top edge of the bag with several rows of machine stitching so it will be secure.

Log Cabin Tablecloth

Tablecloth Size: 56″ × 56″

Content

Top: An assortment of 30 different varieties of cotton and cotton blends (if the color scheme is more limited, make cloth estimates in the usual way—see page 30)

Lining: 3¼ yds. of 36″ cotton seamed down the middle (optional)

Sewing: By machine

Binding: Hemmed

A tablecloth is a simple patchwork project that doesn't require quilting or a lining, although you may add a lining if you wish. The project could also be used as a wall hanging.

This tablecloth is made up of sixteen 14 by 14-inch blocks. The same Log Cabin pattern is used for the tablecloth as for the pocketbook shown on page 53. Follow the directions on page 52 and above for making each block, set the blocks in rows, and then connect the rows. The blocks are set with the dark and the light corners back to back, forming a crosslike design. The setting seams can simply be ironed closed, but for added durability, you may wish to zigzag the edges of each patch before setting, or line the whole tablecloth. When completed, the edges are rolled under and hemmed with a whip stitch (see page 35).

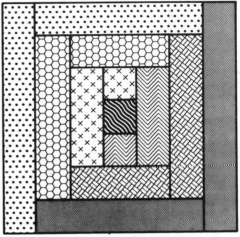

The Log Cabin block design used for the pocketbook shown on page 53 and the tablecloth shown on the facing page. Note the three 2-inch squares in the middle of the block, with the center square brighter than any of the other logs.

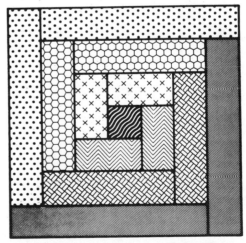

Another way to make a Log Cabin block in the same Dark and Light pattern. The design radiates from a single center square, and the logs overlap each other, rotating clockwise.

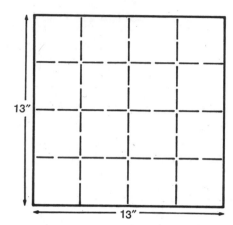

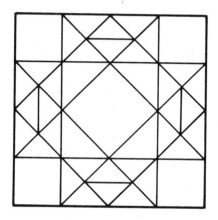

(Above) Sixteen-patch block for drawing the Georgetown Circle block design shown below. Note the four basic pattern shapes of the block design: the large center square, the smaller corner squares, the large center triangles, and the smaller border triangles.

Georgetown Circle Pillow

Pillow Size: 13″ × 13″

Content

Top: 4 silk neckties; ¼ yd. iron-on bonding material
Filling: ½ yd. muslin for inner bag and enough shredded dacron polyester fiberfill to fill it (save scraps from quilting)
Back: ½ yd. silk
Zipper: 12″ neckline or skirt zipper

The Georgetown Circle Pillow has a muslin inner bag to hold the stuffing; using a zipper makes it easy to remove the cover for cleaning.

This is a classic geometric block design. The pattern used here is made from a 13 by 13-inch square, but the pattern can be made any size you wish. Fold a square of paper in half, in half again, and then into quarters, and draw the design by connecting the points resulting from the folds (see diagrams at left).

Patterns. The block is made up of four basic shapes: the middle square, the smaller corner squares, and two triangles of different sizes. Simply transfer one of each of these four shapes to cardboard, adding ¼ inch all around for seam allowances.

Cutting. This pillow, pictured on page 53, was made with four different patterns of silk from neckties. Each tie was opened and ironed to bonding material before it was cut, to prevent fraying. (If you, too, plan to use silk, be sure to bond it with a commercial bonding fabric before you cut out your pattern pieces; most other fabric does not require bonding.)

Sewing. The Georgetown Circle is sewn in the same fashion as most other geometric blocks: Small pieces are sewn into larger units, and the units are then sewn together. Letters refer to the schematic diagrams on the facing page, which show the order in which the pieces are assembled. (Seam allowances are not shown.)

a. Sew the four large triangles to the sides of the center square (see diagram **a**) and put this unit aside. (Refer to the diagram on page 35 for sewing triangles to square.)

b. Next, make four rectangular composites of eight small triangles each. To make each composite, first sew two center triangles together. Then sew a triangle to each side of this center pair to make a pyramid shape. Put this unit aside and sew two pairs of corner triangles. Then join the corner triangles to the pyramid shape, forming a rectangle.

c. Sew corner squares to both sides of two of these rectangular composites. Set aside.

d. Sew the other two rectangular composites to both sides of the large square made in step **a**, forming a large rectangle.

e. Attach the two composites made in step **c** to the top and bottom of this large rectangle with two long seams. Iron all seams closed.

SEWING THE GEORGETOWN CIRCLE

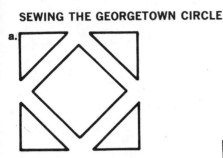

a. Sew large triangles to center square, making a larger square.

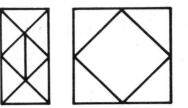

b. Sew four rectangular composites.

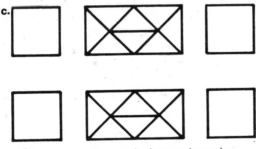

c. Sew corner squares to two rectangular composites.

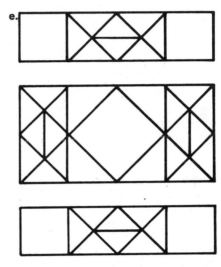

d. Attach other two rectangular composites to large square made in step **a.**

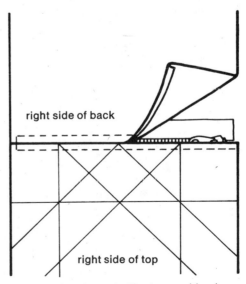

e. Attach two rectangular composites made in step **c** to complete the block.

Iron the patchwork block and use it for a pattern to cut a back for the pillow and two squares of muslin for the inner bag.

Crease and iron under a ¼-inch seam on the right sides of both the patchwork top and the back. Place the top and the back next to each other with right sides facing up. Center and pin the zipper underneath the seams so that the edges of the top and the back of the pillow just meet. Baste the zipper as illustrated in the diagram at right. The seam will be about 3/16 inch from the edges. Use the zipper foot on your sewing machine and sew in the zipper following the basting lines.

Open the zipper and fold both sides of the pillow so that the right sides are facing one another. Baste or pin the edges, beginning at the zipper end, to make sure the edges are even. Sew the remaining three sides and the corners of the top (you may need to hand stitch here); turn the pillow right side out through the open zipper end.

Inner bag. Make the bag for the filling the same size as the pillow cover and drop it in. Stuff more filling in the bag than you think you need, because the filling tends to compress after the pillow is used.

right side of back

right side of top

Basting the zipper to the top and back of the pillow cover

Random-color Squares Quilt

Quilt Size: 63½″ × 74½″ (4″ squares) for a 33″ × 66″ youth bed
Content
Top: At least 4 yds. 45″ cotton or cotton blends in as many colors
      as you wish
Filling: 1½ lbs. or a double layer of 79″ × 90″ dacron polyester
      fiberfill
Back: 4 yds. 45″ cotton flannel
Binding and Border Squares: 2 yds. 45″ cotton
Ties: String, wool yarn, or embroidery floss
Sewing: By machine

Quilting: By tying

Binding: Bias binding

This allover design quilt is made of 4-inch squares. The squares
are set in long rows and the rows are then set diagonally. To
draft a quilt like this, you must draw the outline of the quilt on a
diagonal on graph paper, so that you can draw the squares straight
up and down (see the draft here). Since setting the squares diagonally
results in a saw-toothed edge that would be extremely difficult to
bind, half squares (triangles) were added to make the edges straight.

You can make a similar quilt using different size squares by
following the directions below.

First, decide on the size quilt you would like and the size
squares you want to use. To determine how many squares will be
needed for your quilt, measure out one square on a piece of paper
and measure its diagonal (across the square from corner to corner).
Then divide this measurement into the width and length of the
quilt you are planning. For example, if you wish to use 4-inch
squares, as in this quilt, and you want your quilt to be about 64
by 75 inches, measure the diagonal of a 4-inch square (approximately
5½ inches) and divide first the width (64 inches) and then the
length (75 inches) by this number. This will give you the number
of squares running widthwise (approximately 11½) and lengthwise
(about 13½). Since you don't want to wind up with a fraction of a
square, round off to the nearest number (and adjust your quilt size
accordingly). In this case, round off to 11 squares running widthwise
and 13 squares running lengthwise. Multiply these two numbers
together and multiply by 2 to get the total number of squares you
will need for your quilt—286. (The adjusted quilt size will be approximately 63½ × 74½ inches.)

To experiment with color before making your quilt, draw a draft
of the quilt on graph paper, using colored pencils or markers. Then
calculate your yardage (see page 30), prepare a cardboard pattern
¼ inch larger all around than your desired square size (for seam
allowances), and mark and cut your squares.

Sewing. Lay your squares out on a large flat surface to decide on
the arrangement. Stack the squares in order in diagonal rows, one
row at a time, and sew each row together into long strips by machine.

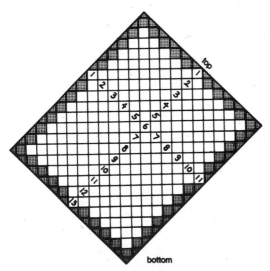

Draft for Random-color Squares quilt
drawn *diagonally* on graph paper with
the squares running straight up and
down; the squares will be set diagonally.
The border squares and triangles are
shaded to indicate that they are all of
the same purple cotton.

"Anna's Quilt." This Random-color Squares quilt is tied with pink cotton string at the corners of the squares.

Each row should be returned to its place until you have sewn all the rows. If you must pick up the squares during this step, mark the rows or stacks of squares with numbers so you can put them back in the right place.

Press each row on the wrong side with the seams all going one way. Set the rows by sewing the strips into groups of two, three, four, and so on. In each case, start sewing from the center of the strip and sew to one edge, then start back at the center of the strip and sew to the other edge (see Setting, page 35).

Tying. Tying is marvelously quick, and easier than other methods of connecting the layers of your quilt if it is especially thick or puffy. The yarn can be tied on either the top or the back of the quilt.

Prepare your quilt for tying by basting the layers together as you would for other methods of quilting (see page 41). The filling should be 1½ inches larger all around than the top or bottom so that you can make a puffy binding. If you have a frame, use it. Cut a long piece of string or wool yarn and thread one length on a large-eyed darning needle. Starting in the center of the quilt, stitch from the top to the back, keeping 2 inches of string on the top. Take a ⅛-inch stitch through the back of the quilt and come back to the top. Tie a square knot and then cut the ends of the string (see diagram). Ties are generally placed in the middle of patches or at seam junctions. They can be placed up to 9 inches apart.

Binding. This quilt is bound with bias strips. A description of the method can be found on page 45.

Alternate method for tying. With this method, the quilt is sewn up on three sides, inside out, and then turned and tied.

First baste the filling to the reverse side of the top, using long diagonal rows of stitching. Keep the top right side up while basting, to avoid creases. Then place the right sides of the top and the back together and baste them together along three of the outer edges. (The quilt will be inside out.) Machine stitch these three edges and turn the quilt right side out through the open side. Tie the quilt, turn the raw edges of the open side in, and whip stitch them together (see page 35). With this method there is no need for a binding.

A square knot: Tie the yarn right over left, then left over right, *then* cut.

Pre-stuffed Triangles Quilt

Quilt Size: 70″ × 98″

Content

Top: 4 yds. denim; 2 yds. blue bandanna-print cotton; 63 large
triangles and 14 small triangles cut from 6 bandannas of various colors

Filling: 3 lbs. or two 81″ × 96″ sheets of dacron polyester fiberfill

Back: 4 yds. each of red and blue bandanna-print cotton

Binding: Blue bandanna-print cotton (left over after cutting triangles)

Sewing: By machine

Binding: Straight-cut binding with squared corners

The pre-stuffing method eliminates the need for overall quilting,
as it combines sewing with stuffing and gives the impression of quilting. It is a fast, effective method of making a patchwork quilt, and
is best suited to large designs. Since there are seams between the
blocks or patches, blocks that are too small would make the quilt
rather stiff, so it is best to make blocks of at least 8 inches on each
side. (On the other hand, blocks should not be larger than 12
inches for squares or 15 inches in altitude for triangles, or the filling
material will bunch. Narrow stripes can be any length you wish.)

Because the stitching in this type of quilt does not go through
the filling but around it, the technique lends itself to puffy, sculptural
quilts. The use of machine stitching makes this sort of quilt very
durable.

Patterns. The draft for this quilt is shown below. The same pattern is used for the top and the back. Two basic pattern pieces,
a large triangle for the body of the quilt and a small one (actually
half the larger one) for the border of the quilt, are needed. First

Drafts for Pre-stuffed Triangles quilt.
Tracing paper was placed over the line
draft to work out the color arrangement.

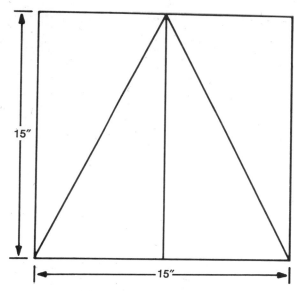

The triangle pattern

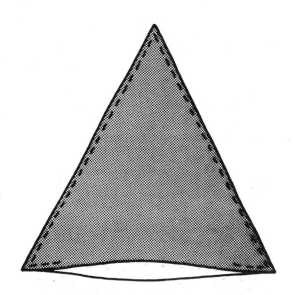

Sew each triangle unit together as illustrated, leaving an opening for stuffing.

Stuff each triangle and then stitch the triangle closed.

draw a 15-inch square on cardboard (see diagram). Find the center of the top side of the square, and draw a line from each bottom corner to this top center point. This will give you your large 15-inch triangle (the seam allowance for this pattern is ½ inch, so the triangle, when sewn, will be a 14-inch triangle). To make the small triangle, cut this pattern piece in half down the center, being sure to allow for ½ inch along the center line for seam allowance.

Mark and cut the triangles for both the front and the back of the quilt—63 large triangles (32 denim and 31 bandanna) and 14 small triangles (6 denim and 8 bandanna); and the same number for the back. Then use the patterns to cut one piece of filling for each triangle unit.

Sewing and stuffing. Put each triangle together with the *wrong* sides of front and back facing. Stitch around three sides, leaving an opening for the stuffing. Insert the stuffing through the open side as illustrated below, and sew the opening closed. (The seam allowance is ½ inch because you stitch each seam twice—once when putting together each triangle and once when connecting the triangles.)

Setting. Connect these triangles as if you were setting any quilt top, by stitching them together in horizontal rows.

You can finish the raw seams that show on the reverse side of the quilt with machine zigzag stitching or hand blanket stitching, or you can sew bias binding over them by hand. The edges of each seam of the quilt illustrated were sewn over with a machine zigzag stitch; the thread matches the red in the quilt.

Binding. Finish the quilt with straight-cut binding (see page 45).

Alternate method for stuffing and setting the triangles. This method is neater but more difficult, because when setting the triangles you must stitch through eight layers of material by hand. Place the *right* sides of the triangles facing each other. Sew them together, leaving an opening. Turn right side out and stuff. Turn a hem under on the edge, and whip stitch the seam. Complete all the triangles in the same manner. To set them, place the right sides of the triangles facing each other and overcast the edges by hand. No binding is needed.

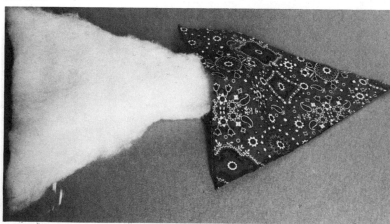

Pre-stuffed Triangles quilt. Note the color arrangement of the triangles and the puffiness of the quilt.

Center Motif Wall Hanging

Wall Hanging Size: 30″ × 30″ octagon

Content

Top: ½ yd. red print cotton; ¼ yd. each of solid-color cotton
Filling: 30″ × 30″ octagonal piece of dacron polyester fiberfill
Back: 1 yd. muslin
Binding: 1 package bias tape

Sewing: By machine

Quilting: By hand

Binding: Bias binding

The Eight-pointed Star design shown here is a little harder to calculate than other designs because you cannot draw it as simply on graph paper. Old-timers probably copied the dimensions of the star from one quilt to another. However, since the design is suitable for a variety of projects, an accurate plan is more practical. An exact one can be drafted from the dimensions of a single diamond-shaped motif, which is repeated over and over to make the star.

Draft. The first step in planning a draft is to decide on the length of the side of the diamond pattern that will be repeated throughout the star. Generally, diamonds range in size from 2½ to 3½ inches long on each side. The side of each diamond in the wall hanging shown here is 3 inches; the side of each point of the star is 9 inches. Each point contains three rows of three diamonds each—nine diamonds. The draft on the left, below, shows two points of the small star plan that is used for the wall hanging, and the draft on the right shows two points of a larger star plan that could be used for a quilt pattern. The two points of both star patterns shown represent one-quarter of an entire star design. It is not necessary to draw an entire draft of a star because the points are all the same.

(Below left) Draft of two points of the Eight-pointed Star wall hanging. (Below right) Expanded draft for two points of an Eight-pointed Star quilt. Directions for drawing both drafts on pages 65–67.

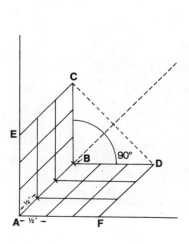

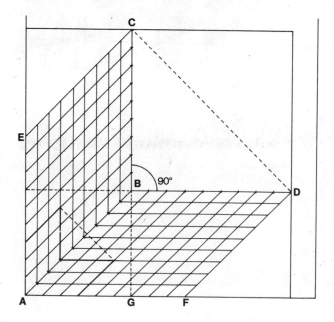

Eight-pointed Star center motif patchwork wall hanging, with gradated color arrangement of plain and printed cotton diamonds.

To draw the draft for the wall hanging, begin by making a diagonal fold (to form a square) in a plain piece of 8½ by 11-inch paper. Then decide on a workable scale. The one used here is ½″ = 3″.

Mark off three ½-inch sections along the diagonal fold (from **A** to **B**). At point **B** draw a 90 degree angle, using either a right angle or the sides of a book. Mark three ½-inch sections along each of these lines (**B** to **C** and **B** to **D**).

Mark three ½-inch sections along the edges of the paper (**A** to **E** and **A** to **F**). Then connect points **C** and **E**, and **D** and **F**, as shown, to form the sides of the star points.

Connect the ½-inch marks, as shown, to form the nine diamonds in each star point.

You can fill in the area between the points of the star either with squares and triangles, which will result in a square wall hanging, or with all triangles, which will result in an octagonal wall hanging like the one shown here. (To find out how big these "fill-in" pieces will be, measure the draft and multiply the dimensions according to your scale.) Finally, place tracing paper over the entire draft to work out your color scheme with pencils or felt-tipped pens.

Quilt Draft. The draft shown on the facing page, right, is for an Eight-pointed Star quilt, like the Lone Star quilt pictured on page 8. This draft is an expanded version of the draft for the wall hanging (which is outlined in the lower left corner). To draw a draft for a star quilt, follow the directions given above for drawing the draft for the wall hanging—but add more diamonds. (Of course, you can adjust your scale and use larger diamonds when you make your quilt, if you wish.) Here, each point of the star quilt contains nine rows of nine diamonds each. So, to start, mark *nine* ½-inch sections along the diagonal fold **AB**. According to the scale used for the wall hanging (½″ = 3″), the side of each point of the star will measure 27 inches.

To find out how large your entire quilt will be (or to find out how large any star project will be), draw a vertical line from point **C** in the draft to the edge of your paper (point **G**). Whether the quilt

DIAMOND PATTERN

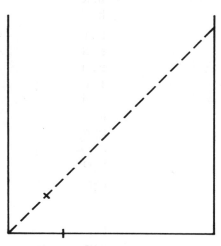

a. Fold 8½ × 11-inch paper on the diagonal, making a square (see page 25).

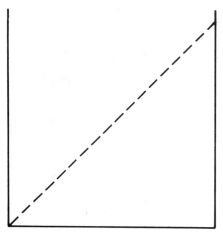

b. Measure and mark 3 inches along side of paper and on folded diagonal line.

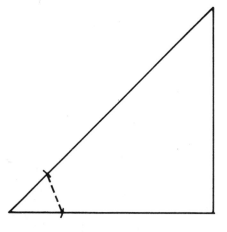

c. Cut out diagonal section, and crease to connect the two 3-inch points.

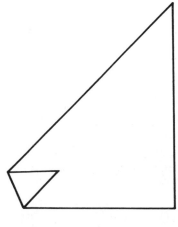

d. Fold the paper over on the crease.

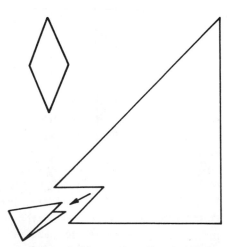

e. Cut out the section that is folded over, open, and you have a diamond.

you are planning is square or octagonal, the length and the width are always equal. So the line **CG** represents half the length (and width) of your quilt. Measure **CG**, multiply according to your scale, and then multiply the result by 2 to get the dimensions of your quilt. For example, if **CG** measures 7 inches, and your scale is ½″ = 3″, then **CG** represents 42 inches. Therefore, the dimensions of your quilt will be 84 by 84 inches.

If your project turns out to be bigger or smaller than you want, either adjust your scale, or add or subtract rows of diamonds.

Patterns: To make the diamond pattern for this wall hanging, see the diagrams and instructions on the facing page. Then outline this pattern on cardboard and add a ¼-inch seam allowance. Draw the patterns for the "fill-in" pieces out on newspaper according to the measurements determined from the draft.

Mark each diamond pattern on the cloth so that two sides run with the grain of the fabric (see photo, below).

Sewing. The star points are pieced separately. First sew the diamonds into rows of three. Sew bias edges to straight edges to prevent stretching. Next sew three rows of diamonds together to make a complete point. After all eight points have been pieced together, connect them into pairs. Sew the pairs together and then sew the two halves of the star into a complete star.

Iron the seams closed on the back so that they fan out from the center. Measure and cut the corner pieces. Start sewing them in place at an outside point and pivot at the corners. Iron again.

Quilting. Use the star block as a pattern to cut the dacron polyester fiberfill and the back. All three layers should be the same size. Baste the layers together. The quilting in this wall hanging outlines some of the diamond shapes. If you want to do extensive quilting, you can outline each diamond shape in each point of the star.

Binding. Finish the edges with bias binding (see page 45).

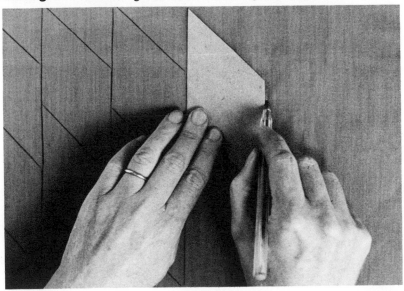

Marking the diamond patterns on cloth

Irregular Design Quilt

Quilt Size: 82″ × 90″ (before stuffing and quilting: 90″ × 90″)

Content

Top: Printed and solid-color cottons (the width of each stripe depends
on the cloth at hand)

Filling: 5 lbs. or three 81″ × 96″ sheets of dacron polyester fiberfill

Back: 6 yds. 45″ cotton flannel

Sewing: By machine

Quilting: By hand

Binding: Self-bound

The combination of stripes of varying widths creates the interesting ridged effect of this quilt. It was made by piecing together scraps into stripes of widths up to 9 inches. Some stripes were made of long strips of very narrow cloth pieced together. Others were made by piecing together ten 9-inch lengths of fabric. Since the width of individual stripes depended on the amount of cloth at hand, a number of cardboard patterns, all 9½ inches long (to accommodate seam allowance), but of varying widths, were moved around the fabric scraps to see which pieces of fabric could be made into which width of stripe.

Once the stripes were sewn and ironed, they were arranged in the order pictured on the facing page, and the top was set.

Stuffing from one open end. The quilt was stuffed from one open end after the top and back had been sewn together on three sides. This method is excellent for stripes or for wave or scallop effects; the stuffing gives a sculptural effect.

Place the top and back of your quilt together with *right* sides facing each other (in other words, your quilt will be inside out). Pin or baste, and machine stitch on three sides. Turn the quilt right side out through the open side. Cut a strip of filling to the width of the first ridge or stripe, and stuff it into the quilt. Pin it in place. Place the quilt on a table so that you can keep one hand underneath it as you sew, and stitch along one side of the ridge, through the top and back. This stitching will hold the filling in place (do not stitch through the filling). Stuff and sew the remaining ridges in the same manner. When you have finished stuffing the quilt, turn the raw edges of the open side in and whip stitch them closed (see page 35).

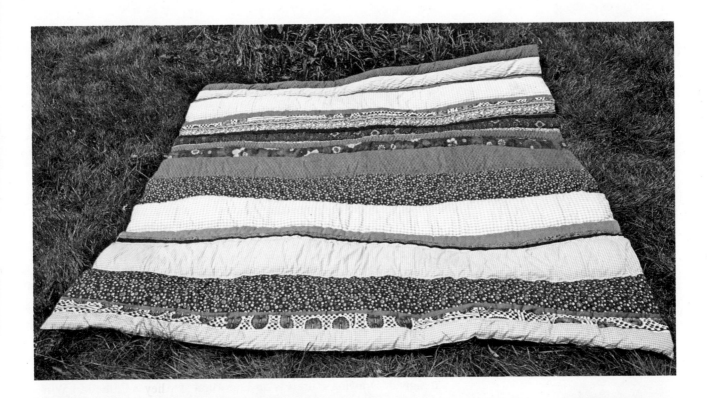

(Top) Irregular Design patchwork quilt. (Bottom) Cathedral Window quilt by Helen Montgomery (see page 70 for instructions). Photo by Daniel Danneman.

The back of the Cathedral Window quilt. Photo by Daniel Danneman.

Cathedral Window Quilt

Quilt Size: 84″ × 99″ (2½″ squares)

Content: 30 yds. 36″ bleached lightweight muslin; miscellaneous cotton prints for the "windows"

Sewing: By hand

A Cathedral Window quilt is made by folding squares of plain cloth to make "frames" for colored or printed cloth "windows." The plain squares are folded separately and then connected to make up the entire quilt, both top and back (there is no filling, and no quilting as such). When the window patches are sewn in through all the folded layers of the plain cloth squares, the stitches give the effect of quilting on the back of the quilt. In the quilt pictured on page 69, the squares are set diagonally. The back, pictured here, shows how the squares look and the quilting effect that results when the print patches are sewn in.

Because the squares are set diagonally, the edge of this quilt is saw-toothed. For a quilt with straight edges, like the one shown on page 12, the squares are set horizontally and vertically. Make a plan on graph paper for the setting method you prefer.

The draft. The illustration of the draft shows how this quilt is designed. Drawing a draft is an important step for a Cathedral Window quilt, because you need to know how many squares there will be in order to purchase enough plain cloth to match throughout the quilt; also, a draft tends to make the sewing method clearer.

Begin the draft in the lower center of the graph paper. For this quilt, one square on the paper equals one folded cloth square 2½ by 2½ inches. The number of squares in each row increases by two squares each row: 1, 3, 5, 7, 9, and so on. So that the quilt will be longer than it is wide, four identical rows are placed at the center (in this case, four rows of 43 squares each). More identical rows would increase the length; fewer rows would make the quilt shorter.

Cloth estimates. There are 1,054 folded squares of plain cloth in this quilt; each is 6 by 6 inches before folding. It is possible to cut thirty-six squares from 1 yard of 36-inch fabric.

The print squares total 2,016. These "windows" are cut from such small bits of cloth of so many varieties (all leftovers) that an estimate is impossible to give. If you need to buy cloth for these pieces, select as large a variety as you can—much of the beauty of this quilt comes from the sparkling effect of many colors of cloth.

Patterns. Cut a 6-inch square cardboard pattern for the plain cloth and a 1½-inch square for the colored cloth. Mark and cut the cloth. Then follow the instructions given with the step-by-step photographs that begin on the facing page.

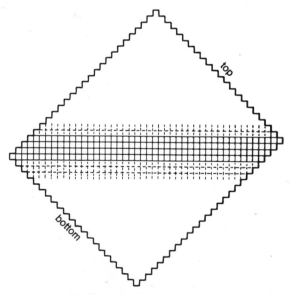

Draft of Cathedral Window quilt. There are four equal rows of 43 squares each in the center of the quilt.

STEPS FOR CATHEDRAL WINDOW QUILT

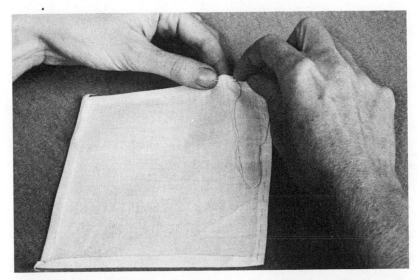

a. Fold in the edges of the 6-inch plain cloth squares ¼ inch, and baste.

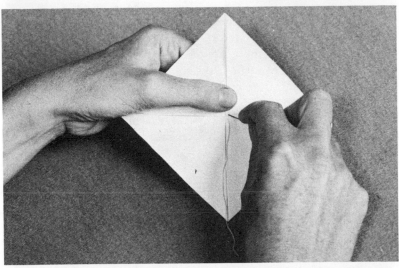

b. Fold all four corners to the center. Press the folds and tack the center corners down by stitching through the corners and the back with several overlapping stitches.

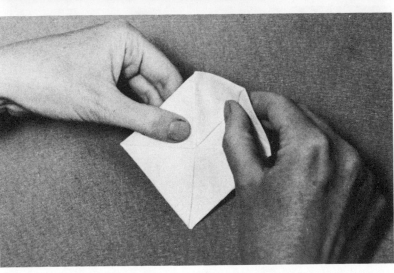

c. Fold the corners of this square to the center again. Press. Tack the corners down with overlapping stitches. This is the basic unit for the quilt. Make nine of these 2½ by 2½-inch squares to start.

d. Each row increases in length by two squares: 1, 3, 5, and so on. Put the first square (the first "row") aside and make rows of three and five squares: Place the *backs* of the squares facing one another and overcast a row of stitches to connect the sides. Make the stitches very close so the quilt will be sturdy. Then open both rows flat. Place the single square back to back with the center square of the row with three squares. Overcast and open this section. Overcast the row of five squares to the row of three squares and open the entire section.

e. The colored "window" squares are placed on top of and between two plain ones. Place a colored square carefully between two plain ones, pin it in place, and bring the adjacent folded edges of the two plain squares around and over the raw edges of the colored one; whip stitch in place. (Make sure your stitches go all the way through the back to create the quilting effect.)

f. Continue to add rows of squares until you reach the midpoint; put this section aside. Start again from the opposite corner (the bottom corner of the quilt) and construct the other half of the quilt. When both of these sections are complete, overcast the center seam, finishing the quilt. The folding process produces a finished edge, so there is no need for binding. The photo at right by Daniel Danneman shows a detail of the finished quilt.

Crazy Quilt Wall Hanging

Block Size: 21″ × 21″

Content

Top: ¾ yd. muslin; miscellaneous scraps of silk, velvet, wool, and corduroy

Back: ¾ yd. wool flannel (corduroy or sailcloth would be acceptable as well)

Embroidery: Yarn or embroidery floss

Sewing: By hand

Binding: Self-bound

The method used for this wall hanging is a combination of appliqué and embroidery. The odd-shaped scraps of fabric are fitted together onto a 20 by 20-inch muslin backing; then the edges of the scraps are turned under 3/16 inch and whip stitched down (see page 35). The pieces of the crazy quilt block must fit together like the pieces of a jigsaw puzzle, with whipped edges overlapping raw ones. In the block pictured here, the seams are stitched over with a decorative feather stitch (see diagram) in various colors of yarn. Last, a 22½ by 22½-inch back is attached, and the edges of the back are turned over the top for a self binding (see directions for using the back as binding on page 43).

To make an entire crazy quilt, assemble as many of the blocks described above as you need for the quilt size you have chosen.

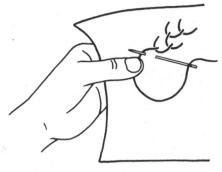

Feather stitch. Alternate the stitch from one side of a center line to the other (in this project, the seam lines). Hold the loop of the thread with your thumb, so that the thread is *under* the needle point when you take a stitch.

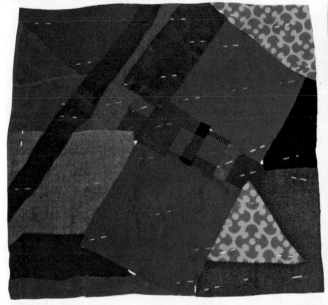 

(Left) Crazy quilt pieces fitted together and pinned in place. (Right) The finished wall hanging has colorful yarn ties; the seams are finished with a decorative feather stitch.

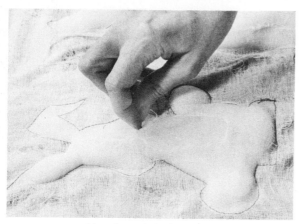

Mending the slits after the pockets have been stuffed

Trapunto Quilt

Quilt Size: 70″ × 88″

Content

Top: 2 yds. 54″ cotton; 4 yds. 36″ cheesecloth

Filling: 54″ × 72″ piece of dacron polyester fiberfill; pieces of fiberfill for stuffing

Back: 4 yds. 36″ cotton flannel

Border and Ruffle: ¼ yd. cotton for narrow border strips; 1½ yds. cotton for bottom ruffle and wide top border strip; 2 yds. cotton for the side ruffles

Ties: Assorted colored yarn or string

Sewing: By machine

Quilting: By machine and by tying

Binding: A border and ruffles are added; the quilt is not bound

Trapunto-style child's quilt

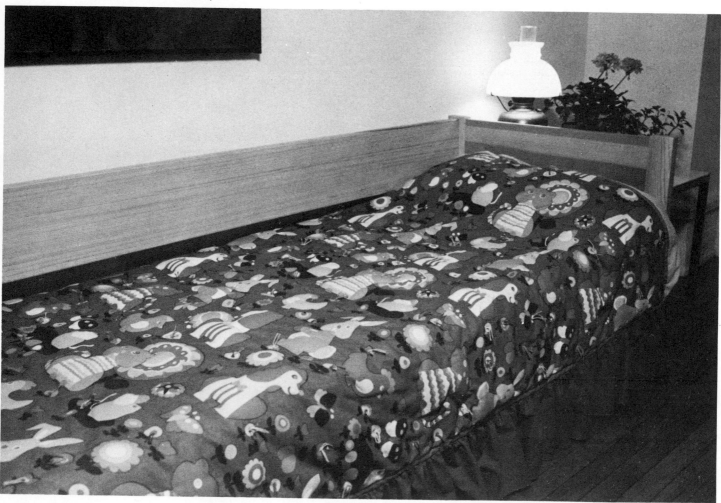

In this contemporary adaptation of the classic hand-sewn trapunto quilt, the quilting follows the printed design of the cloth on the top. This quilting technique is suitable for block quilts as well as for one-piece tops.

Assemble the cheesecloth so that it is the same size as the quilt top (in this case, 54 by 72 inches), and baste it to the reverse side of the top with straight vertical rows of stitching. Since cheesecloth is stretchy, smooth and baste every 6 inches.

Next, machine stitch areas of the top to create pockets for the stuffing. In this project the quilt stitching outlines the animals printed on the cloth. (You could also draw your own design if you wished.) Follow the design on your cloth top with free-motion machine stitching (see your sewing machine instruction book), or by machine stitching in your usual manner—try both methods to see which one you prefer. Begin sewing at the center of the top and work out to the edges.

Turn the quilt to the cheesecloth side. Cut slits large enough to push pieces of the filling into place. Fill the pockets only enough to make the design puffy—don't pack them too full. Mend the slits closed again with stitches that pull the cheesecloth back together (see photo on the facing page). Don't worry about mending the slits neatly—the lining will cover the cheesecloth. When all the pockets have been stuffed, cut slices in the cheesecloth parallel to and around the stuffing to release the tension and to keep the cloth from puckering. Iron the top, especially around the stuffed designs.

Add the border and the ruffles to the top. Cut and piece four 1-inch strips—two strips that are 1 by 56 inches for the top and bottom of the quilt and two strips that are 1 by 74 inches for the sides. Pin the border to the top of the quilt, right sides together, making squared corners (see top diagram). Stitch the border to the quilt ¼″ from the edge, and iron the quilt top.

Cut an 8 by 56-inch strip for the wide top border (the top has no ruffle). Cut an 8 by 112-inch strip for the bottom ruffle, and two strips, 8 by 148 inches each, for the two side ruffles. Machine stitch loosely along the edge of each ruffle. Pull one thread to gather each ruffle, and pin them to the border of the quilt, right sides together. Sew the ruffles and the top border to the quilt. Roll and hem each ruffle.

Add a layer of dacron polyester fiberfill for additional warmth, and then add the back. Cut the back 2 inches larger all around than the top (in this case the back is 56 by 74 inches). The back will cover the rough seams of the border and the ruffle. Turn the edges of the back over the border and ruffle seams (see bottom diagram), and whip stitch the back down. Tie the layers of the quilt together with colorful string ties. (For directions on tying, see page 60.)

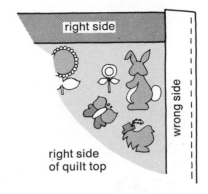

The border of this trapunto quilt is attached in the same way as straight-cut binding (see page 45).

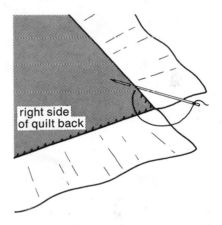

Turn a hem, and then whip stitch the back of the quilt over the unfinished edges of the border and the ruffle.

(Above) Appliqué presentation quilt with 25 different bird blocks. (Facing page, top) Redwing Blackbird block by Ginger Hill. Note the elaborate background quilting. (Middle) Seagull block by Carol Tomson. (Bottom) This signature label includes the names of everyone who made a bird block, and is sewn to the back of the quilt. The Scarlet Tanager block shown on the back cover is by Grace Meyer.

Appliqué Presentation Quilt

Quilt Size: 72″ × 72″ (12″ squares)

Content

Top: 3 yds. 45″ permanent-press muslin for twenty-two 13″ squares; ½ yd. cotton for three 13″ squares (the assortment for the appliqués is impossible to estimate); 2 yds. 45″ cotton for 60 lattice strips, 2½″ × 13″; ¼ yd. cotton for thirty-six 2½″ corner squares

Filling: Twenty-five 13½″ squares of dacron polyester fiberfill (cut from a double bed-size sheet)

Back: 9 yds. 36″ cotton for twenty-five 18″ squares

Sewing: By hand

Quilting: By hand

Binding: Self-bound

This contemporary example of the classic presentation quilt is an illustration of the versatility of appliqué, the most pictorial of all quiltmaking techniques. The appliqués of American birds are set against squares of unbleached muslin and light violet cotton. The background colors and the various fabrics for the appliquéd birds were distributed throughout the quilt so that there would be as little repetition of color as possible, while maintaining an overall unified effect. Since subtle variations of color are impossible with cloth, the effect is a stylized one.

A number of people made and quilted the squares for this quilt. Working on a group project such as this one is a good way to begin appliquéing, since it gives everyone who works on it the opportunity to experiment on a small scale. After all the squares were completed, the quilt was assembled, and it now circulates among the people who made the squares. Other possible subjects for group quilting projects include wild flowers, trees, animals, historic scenes, and special occasions and events.

This quilt is meant to be a wall hanging, so it has rings across the top for hanging and a casing for a rod (to keep it hanging straight).

Sewing. Cut twenty-five 13-inch squares. (The finished squares will be 12 by 12 inches; there is a ½-inch seam allowance for connecting the squares.) Make a paper pattern for each bird shape, allowing for a 3/16-inch hem, and then cut the pattern apart according to color. (Pictures of birds were used for these patterns.) Cut the cloth for the pieces out of the colors you have chosen, remembering to allow for 3/16-inch hems, and cut little V-shaped notches at ¼-inch intervals around all curved edges.

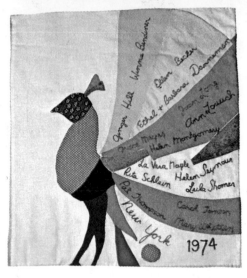

Pin the appliqué pieces to the backing squares and sew them down with a whip stitch (see page 35). Use thread to match the colors of the appliqués. Turn the 3/16-inch hems under as you sew. You can overlap raw edges with folded ones, and embellish your stitching with embroidery if you wish (see the section on appliqué, page 35).

Iron the squares.

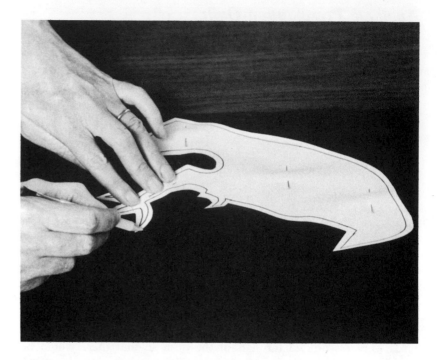

Marking around a bird pattern (the crow). Note the double outline for the seam allowance.

Quilting the squares. Cut a 13½-inch square of filling and an 18-inch square for the back of each block. Stack the top, filling, and back of each square together, and baste with a corner-to-corner X. Quilt each square individually, by hand. Since these squares are so small, it is not necessary to use a quilting hoop.

Setting. This quilt is set with lattice strips 2½ by 13 inches. The lattice strips are sewn to the sides of each square using the method for Quilting by Sections described on page 41. After the squares have been connected with lattice strips, the quilt is turned to the back and the filling is evened and cut where it overlaps. The back sections are also cut even and finished with the edge of one side overlapping the next side; each seam is turned under and whip stitched. The small colored squares at the corners of each block are applied last. Crease and iron a ¼-inch hem around each of these squares. They are then laid on to the corners with a whip stitch that goes through all the layers of the quilt.

Binding. This quilt is self-bound. The top and back outside edges of the quilt are turned in and slip stitched closed as described on page 42.

Care and Restoration

WASHING

New machine-stitched, dacron-filled quilts may be washed by machine and dried in an automatic dryer. Front-loading machines seem to be easier on quilts than machines with center agitators. Use the "gentle" setting.

Hand-stitched quilts, or old quilts filled with cotton batting, should not be machine washed. If you have such a quilt, wash it in a bathtub, using cool water and mild soap. Squeeze the water out, wrap the quilt in towels, and dry it in a shady place. You may hang the quilt over the dowel from your quilting frame, over a doubled clothesline, or lay it on a sheet on the grass to dry.

FOLDING AND STORING

If you store a quilt for a long period of time, re-fold it from time to time or the folds will become worn. If you live in a wet climate, keep your quilt in a dry place to keep it from getting moldy.

REPAIRS

Antique quilts often have worn spots; many old quilts were made from used cloth to begin with. It is not difficult to replace old patches with new ones by appliquéing. If the cloth for your new patches is too bright for the cloth of your old quilt, use the wrong side, or fade it by soaking it in a weak solution of bleach.

Quilt Collections

The following is a partial list of museum collections featuring quilts. Since their collections are not always on display, and not all museums are easily accessible, you may want to write to them for catalogs, pamphlets, books, and other information on their collections.

Bookshop
Denver Art Museum
100 West 14th Avenue Parkway
Denver, Colorado 80204

Academy Shop
Honolulu Academy of Arts
900 South Beretania Street
Honolulu, Hawaii 96814

The University of Kansas Museum
  of Art
Lawrence, Kansas 66044

The Baltimore Museum of Art
Department of Textiles
Art Museum Drive
Baltimore, Maryland 21218

Curator of Decorative Arts
The Newark Museum
43 Washington Street
Newark, New Jersey 07101

Research Department
Shelburne Museum
Shelburne, Vermont 05482

Bibliography

"American Pieced Quilts," Introduction by Jonathon Holstein, The Smithsonian Institution Traveling Exhibition, Washington, D.C., 1972.

Colby, Averil, *Quilting.* Charles Scribner's Sons, New York, New York, 1971.

Ickis, Marguerite, *The Standard Book of Quilt-Making and Collecting.* Reprinted by Peter Smith Publisher, Inc., Gloucester, Massachusetts, 1973.

Laury, Jean R., *Quilts and Coverlets, A Contemporary Approach.* Van Nostrand Reinhold Co., New York, New York, 1970.

Leman, Bonnie, *Quick and Easy Quilting.* Hearthside Press, Inc., Great Neck, New York, 1972.

———, ed., "Quilter's Newsletter." For subscription information, write to Box 394, Wheat Ridge, Colorado 80033.

Lewis, Alfred A., *The Mountain Artisans Quilting Book.* Macmillan Publishing Co., Inc., New York, New York, 1973.

McKim, Ruby S., *One Hundred and One Patchwork Patterns.* Rev. ed., Dover Publications, Inc., New York, New York, 1962; Peter Smith Publisher, Inc., Gloucester, Massachusetts, 1973.

Wooster, Ann-Sargent, *Quiltmaking, The Modern Approach to a Traditional Craft.* Drake Publishers, Inc., New York, New York, 1972.

Appliqué and stitchery medallion-center cushion by Virginia Davis. The area surrounding the medallion is hand quilted.

Suppliers

Most of the tools and materials mentioned in this book are readily available at local needlecraft and fabric shops and at large department stores. The following is a partial list of suppliers from whom you can order by mail. Unless otherwise noted, all carry general supplies (filling, hoops, frames, and so on), and many carry fabrics, quilt plans, and quilting patterns as well.

Herrschners, Inc.
Hoover Rd.
Stevens Point, Wis. 54481

H. Houst and Son
Woodstock, N.Y. 12498
(silicone-coated quilting thread)

Mary Maxim
2001 Holland Ave.
Port Huron, Mich. 48060

Merribee Needlecraft Co.
2904 W. Lancaster St.
P.O. Box 9680
Fort Worth, Tex. 76107

Needleart Guild
2729 Oakwood Ave., N.E.
Grand Rapids, Mich. 49505

Sears, Roebuck and Co.
(contact the nearest Sears store for catalog)

The Stearns and Foster Co.
Quilt Dept., Lockland
Cincinnati, Ohio 45215

Quilting Services
(groups that will hand quilt a finished top)

Cabin Creek Quilts
P.O. Box 383
Cabin Creek, W. Va. 25035

Senior Citizens Industries
P.O. Box 1302
Grand Island, Neb. 68801

The Stearns and Foster Co.
Quilt Dept., Lockland
Cincinnati, Ohio 45215